A Knitter's Guide to
Gloves

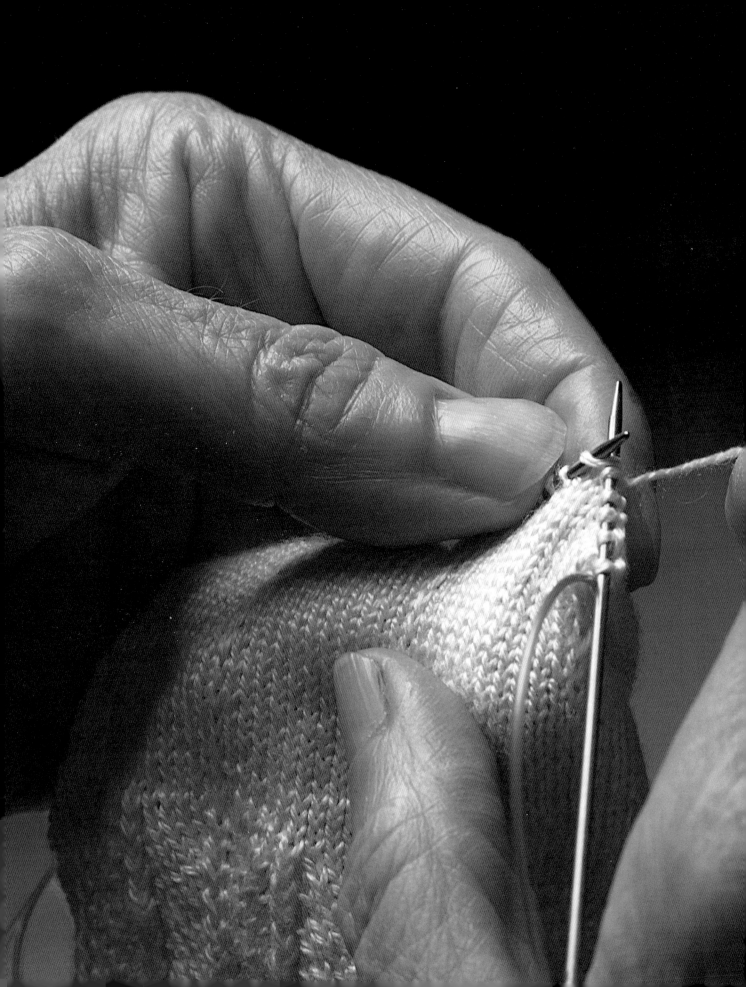

Angharad Thomas

A Knitter's Guide to
Gloves

THE CROWOOD PRESS

First published in 2023 by
The Crowood Press Ltd
Ramsbury, Marlborough
Wiltshire SN8 2HR

enquiries@crowood.com
www.crowood.com

British Library Cataloguing-in-Publication Data
A catalogue record for this book is available from the British Library.

ISBN 978 0 71984172 9

Cover design: Sergey Tsvetkov
Frontispiece: Geof Cunningham

Dedication

To Mary Allen of Dent and Mary Forsyth of Sanquhar, glove knitters

Typeset by Chennai Publishing Services
Printed and bound in India by Parksons Graphics

CONTENTS

Introduction   7

1	Understanding Glove Knitting	9
	Pattern 1: Plain Inspired	30
2	A History of Knitting or a History of Knitted Gloves?	33
	Pattern 2: Inspired by History	50
3	Patterned Gloves in Yorkshire, Scotland and Estonia	55
	Pattern 3: Inspired by Mary Allen	65
	Pattern 4: Inspired by Alba	77
	Pattern 5: Boreal Inspiration	88
4	Get Creative: Design for Glove Knitters	93
5	Knitted Gloves in Collections	117
	Pattern 6: Vintage Inspiration	128

Appendix I: Abbreviations   133

Appendix II: Alphabet Charts   134

Bibliography   135

Resources   137

Acknowledgements   140

Index   141

BT 86·3·22

INTRODUCTION

This book is about knitted gloves. It's a lot about knitting and it's a lot about gloves. Both are fascinating, so together they must be even more so. Some of it is relevant for knitting of any kind. Why gloves? Why not hats or socks, as surely they are easier to knit? And can't warm, hardwearing gloves be bought for a small amount of money almost anywhere? So why knit them?

Knitting has been a fascination of mine for most of my life, and at times also my employment. I am a hand and machine knitter, and use either as the task demands. Knitted gloves have been part of my knitting repertoire since I started to make them about forty years ago, using patterns in *Patons Woolcraft*, that long-lasting staple of instruction and basic patterns. At that time, because I was a knitter, a friend gave me a pair of gloves, finely hand knitted in grey and red wool, shown in the illustration, which she said had come from her aunt who kept a post office in the Yorkshire Dales. These gloves fascinated me as I had never seen knitting so fine and so patterned – and that must have been the beginning of my obsession!

Gloves – that is, hand coverings with separate fingers – have been found throughout recorded time, and making gloves, whether from fabric or skins, has continued ever since. The name for this hand covering with separate fingers is said to have various roots; however, my favourite is that the word 'glove' came from an old Belgic word *gheloove*, meaning faithfulness, as gloves have been so strongly associated with love tokens.

For me, the interest in gloves lies in the endless variations: as protection from cold or hazards, as decoration or status symbol, as part of a uniform, as part of sports kit – all these are possibilities for the glove. A glove can be the most exquisite work of craft and skill decorated with precious metals and jewels, or it can be see-through plastic of the sort that is given out at the petrol station or with hair dye, or to protect the hand from contamination during a pandemic. Gloves might be worn to protect the hands from irreparable damage in severe climates, or they might be of diaphanous lace covering the hands and arms, the only intention being decoration. Given the many uses to which a glove or gloves can be put, the many materials that gloves can be made from, and the differing resources that may be used in glove manufacture, this variety is probably infinite.

Religious writings, myths, legends, the Greeks and Romans, not to mention Shakespeare, all refer to gloves. Shakespeare was close to gloves, being the son of a glove maker, whose workshop can be seen in his home town of Stratford-upon-Avon, England. It would be natural to him to be familiar with the 'language' of gloves. In the other contexts, from earliest times, gloves are given as tokens of affection, they are passed around with money in them, they are worn on hats as a signal of loyalty, and they are perfumed and given as gifts. They may or may not be worn, depending on particular circumstances. Judges wore white gloves when there were no instances of the death penalty in that session of the court, and there was a period when Wales was known as the 'land of white gloves'. Gloves were apparently given as gifts to attendees of weddings and funerals.

These customs are recorded and found all over Europe, and were actively used or performed until relatively recently. Some associations still continue in modern form, such as the contemporary furniture removal firm that reassures prospective customers with its title of 'White Glove Removals', indicating the level of care that will be taken.

References to gloves permeate our speech, from phrases such as 'hand in glove', 'throwing down the gauntlet', 'quirk' (a small piece of a leather glove that enables the finger to fit well), 'fit like a glove', and 'the gloves are off'.

Despite the warming climate, our sedentary indoor lifestyles, central heating, use of the car and so on, gloves are still part of daily life, whether it's for doing the washing up, for gardening, or when going out for a brisk, life-enhancing walk in nature! That's where a pair of cosy hand-knitted gloves might come in handy! (Absolutely no pun intended!)

I hope this book conveys to you, the reader, just a fraction of the interest and excitement I have had from making, designing and studying knitted gloves, this extremely niche textile activity.

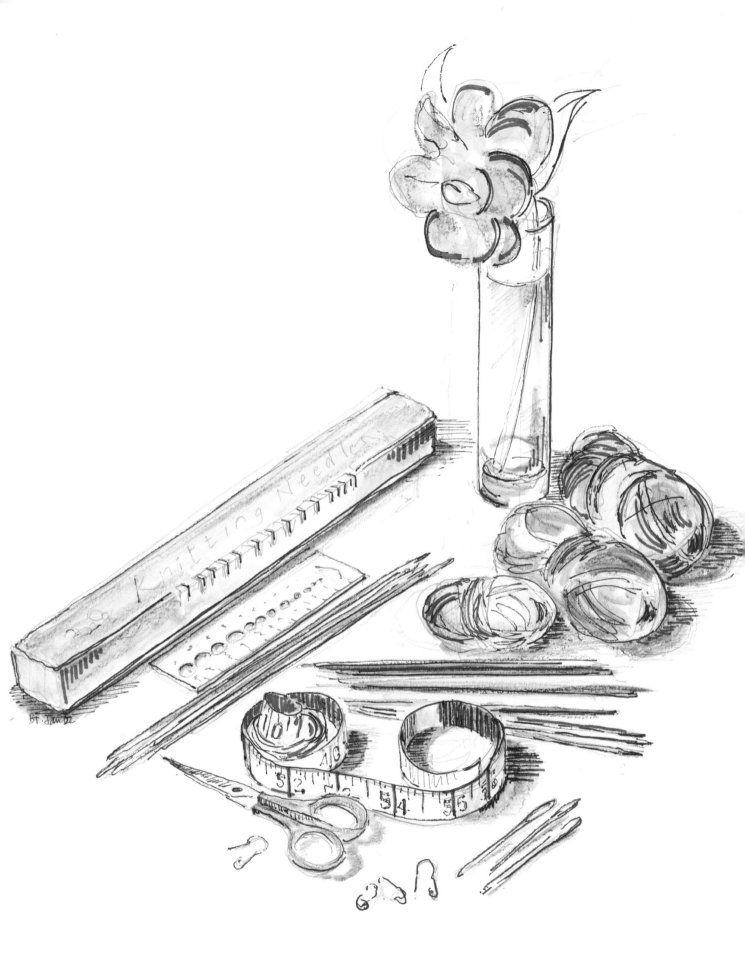

UNDERSTANDING GLOVE KNITTING

Background: Why Gloves?

The Significance of Gloves

Gloves come in a vast range of types, either functional or decorative, or both in some cases. Gloves can protect the hands from dirt or germs, can insulate them from extreme temperatures, whether high or low, or give protection from danger in a work context and on the sportsfield. From delicate lace gloves, which can be knitted or crocheted, to embroidered gloves made from the finest materials for ceremonial occasions, or elbow-length evening gloves or chic leather gloves for driving, the whole spectrum of style is to be found. Gloves have a place in the English language too. We use phrases such as 'hand in glove', 'fits like a glove' or 'taking the gloves off' to add weight and colour to our meanings. Gloves have been used over the centuries as tokens of power or love, and later in this book examples of gloves used in these ways are shown.

The oldest pair of gloves in existence are those that were discovered in the tomb of the Egyptian king Tutankhamun, dating back over 3,000 years. It must be emphasized, however, that these were not knitted. Chapter 2 gives an outline of the history of the glove as an item of clothing, where it will be seen that the knitted form appears quite late on.

Gloves Expressing Feelings – Exploring Relationships

Perhaps because of the immense possibility of variation in the glove form, briefly discussed above, and because of its close relationship with the human hand, gloves have been used in both fine art and craft contexts to explore specific questions or feelings by makers in recent years. British artists Rozanne Hawksley and Alice Kettle have employed gloves to great effect in their textile pieces during their careers.

Rozanne Hawksley has used gloves in her constructed textile works over a period of many years, and the importance of the glove in her work as a symbol and motif is reflected by its presence in the Glove Collection Trust, the collection that has its origins in the Worshipful Company of Glovers of London. Five of Rozanne Hawksley's pieces that feature gloves are to be seen as part of this collection on its website (*see* Resources section at the back of this book). All use the glove form, three with a large, flared gauntlet, heavily ornamented and decorated, in the way that gloves were constructed historically, and two using the form of long, white, formal gloves as the basis for the artwork. However, the message of power and status is then subverted by additions such as Tarot cards, small animal skulls, and inscribed ribbon saying things such as 'famine'.

These pieces, which are labelled as 'Sculpture or assembled artwork', use the language of gloves to convey powerful messages, commenting on life, death, and the human condition. Other pieces use large numbers of gloves in wreath shapes to give messages about the futility of war and the need for peace. Some of these are in the collection of the Imperial War Museum, London. In a book about Rozanne's work Mary Schoeser says that 'for a number of years [she has been] using the glove as the symbol of the human individual' – and Rozanne's work shows this to be a rich seam of visual imagery.

The attraction of gloves is explained by Alice Kettle in her artist's statement for her exhibition 'Telling Fortunes' in Platt Hall Gallery of Costume, Manchester, UK in 2010. She says:

I am amongst many artists who are drawn to gloves. Loaded with the symbolism of touch and the haptic they are suggestive of the movement and gesture of the hand. They carry a sense of changing cultural attitude, when gloves must be worn, of the untouched and must not touch, and of relationships, when hands are to be held. They hold within their interior a sense of the hand within.

Using gloves from the collection held at Platt Hall, her embroidered piece 'Glove Field' outlines many gloves filling a white cotton background that measures 1 × 2m. A central structure in the exhibition had gloves from the Platt Hall collection displayed on it, and other visuals used the outline of the glove as a motif, including on ceramic pieces. These works can be seen on Alice's website (*see* Resources at the back of this book).

Freddie Robins has used the knitted glove form to explore ideas, responding to them in a playful way. Dating from 1997, the series of four knitted gloves shown comment on the form of the hand itself, reacting to and exploring related issues. 'Polly', second from the left, is a comment on the polydactyl condition, when a person may have more than five fingers, while 'Conrad', to the right of it, imagines the consequences of thumb sucking in a German fairytale, which results in the boy's thumb falling off.

Subsequently Robins has knitted gloves that are joined to each other in pairs that would never come apart, some that have small gloves at the tips of the fingers of a larger glove, and some that are joined at the cuffs in a cross form. One series, the 'Hands of Hoxton', commissioned by the London Borough of Shoreditch, matches the gloves to well-known figures from the local area, and this can be seen on the Freddie Robins website (*see* Resources). One of Robins' stated aims with these impossible-to-wear gloves was to get away from the idea that everything 'has to be useful', especially for female makers, for whom this is an additional constraint to female creativity.

'Giles', 'Polly', 'Conrad', 'Peggy', from the series 'Odd Gloves', 1997. Machine-knitted wool, mohair. Approximately 240 × 160mm. 'Giles', 'Polly' and 'Conrad' are in the collection of the Victoria & Albert Museum, London; 'Peggy' is in a private collection. (Ben Coode-Adams)

Types of Hand Covering

The German and Dutch words for glove translate as 'hand shoes' – in other words, a shoe for the hand, and this is what a glove is, in effect. It is a protection or decoration for the hand, in the way that a shoe is for the foot. Passages in the Bible have been thought to refer incorrectly to 'shoes' when they should have referred to 'gloves', so it seems that the connection is close in other languages too. A common definition of 'glove' is a covering for the hand worn for protection against cold or dirt, and typically having separate parts for each finger and the thumb. The forms that hand coverings take can vary widely from, at the simplest, a rectangle of fabric folded in half and sewn up with a gap for the thumb, to a full glove with a gauntlet coming over the wrist; *see* the circular illustration of some of these varieties.

The focus of this book is gloves with full fingers, but any glove pattern can be amended simply by finishing at the level of the knuckles for a fingerless mitt, or turning it into a mitten without separate fingers. Just the cuff and wrist could be made to produce wrist or pulse warmers. For using touch-screen phones and tablets, having finger ends accessible can be an advantage in all but the coldest weather. Gloves are on the market with touch-sensitive areas at the fingertips for use with screens, and conductive thread can be bought for making additions to existing gloves. For artists using screens, gloves consisting of the third and fourth fingers only, which leave the first and second fingers free, are now available, giving yet another permutation of hand covering.

So, with reference to the forms shown, the simplest of these is the wrist warmer, pulse warmer or muffatee, which covers just the wrist area (A). Then the simplest hand warmer is just a tube with a slit for the thumb (B). The form progresses to having a shaped section for the thumb with a separate opening, fingerless mitts (C). Mittens enclose the fingers but keep the thumb separate (D), while a shooting glove or trigger glove has a single finger and a larger space for the other three fingers of the hand (E). Fingerless mitts can be made with a pop-over top allowing some flexibility in use (F), while a fingerless glove has fingers that usually end at the first knuckle (G). A full glove covers the hand while keeping the fingers and thumb separate from each other (H). A glove with a gauntlet comes down over the wrist and part-way up the arm (I). Elbow-length gloves are just as they are described (J).

A Pulse warmer
B Hand warmer
C Fingerless mitten
D Mitten
E Trigger glove
F Mitten with pop over top
G Fingerless glove
H Full glove
I Glove with gauntlet
J Elbow length glove

Types of hand covering.

All these shapes and constructions are related and are relatively easily varied by the maker. For instance, a glove pattern could be used to make most of the variations shown, a possible exception being B, a wrist warmer that is best made from a flat piece of fabric, so that an opening can be left for the thumb, while all the others are easier to make by knitting in the round. All the patterns in this book could be turned into wrist warmers or mittens or fingerless gloves, as preferred. Making adaptations such as this is discussed in Chapter 4. This book takes the full finger glove, H, as its standard model, and all the patterns are for this form of hand covering; however, from this basic shape, the other variations are easily made.

The Anatomy of a Glove

Gloves have particular names for the various parts, these being simplified from the intricate constructions of fabric or leather gloves. Knitted gloves are less complex in their construction as the fabric is stretchy and so accommodates the hand more easily; this is one of the main advantages of using knitting as a glove-making technique. The 'anatomy' of a typical knitted glove is illustrated.

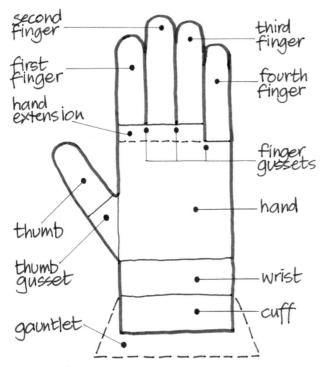

Anatomy of a glove.

Construction usually starts (but does not have to) at the cuff, which, if hand knitted, is often ribbed for a snug fit. Above this, the wrist can be patterned or textured. The shaping to accommodate the thumb, the thumb gusset, then takes shape. In a shaped or gusset thumb, once the stitches for the thumb are formed, they are either taken off and saved to be knitted later, or they can be knitted immediately. Another option is for the thumb to be constructed from a simple slit in the palm of the glove, from which the thumb is knitted up. This is called a peasant thumb. Above this, the hand can again be patterned.

The fourth finger is often knitted first. After it is completed, the hand stitches are returned to and knitted to form the hand extension. This is to take into account the fact that for most people's hands, the start of the fourth or little finger is lower than the others. Note for anxious glove knitters, this is not essential! Knitted gloves have enough stretch and accommodation to allow for this without the hand extension, although it is a nice refinement for ensuring a good fit.

The fingers are formed in turn by taking stitches from either side of the hand and making extra stitches by both casting on and picking up and knitting, to allow for the width of the hands. These stitches can make fully formed finger gussets or fourchettes, or just be a group of several stitches. The fingers are knitted in turn, individually, with the fingertips then shaped to either a blunt or pointed end.

A Little More about Thumb Constructions

The hand of a glove is a cylinder of fabric that wraps around it, but the thumb has to go somewhere and gloves must be constructed to allow for this. It can be done in several ways, and this can be confusing for the beginner glove knitter. However, after having knitted a pair, things should become clearer.

The Position of the Thumb
On the side of the hand: The thumb shaping is positioned between the stitches for the back and the front of the hands, where they meet. Its position on the side of the hand means that both gloves are identical and can be worn on either hand.
    Alternatively:

On the palm of the hand: The thumb shaping is positioned on the palm of the hand, bringing it round to the front of the hand a short way, perhaps a few stitches. This means that the right and left glove are different from each other.

Side thumb, symmetrical.

Peasant thumb, on palm.

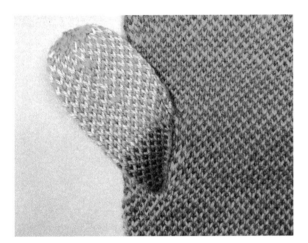

Thumb on palm, symmetrical, showing increases.

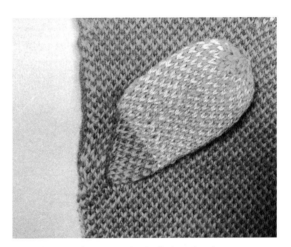

Thumb on palm, symmetrical, showing increases.

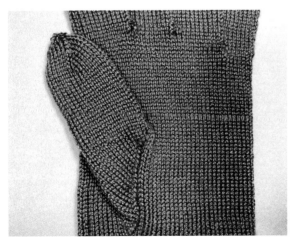

Thumb on palm, asymmetrical, showing increases.

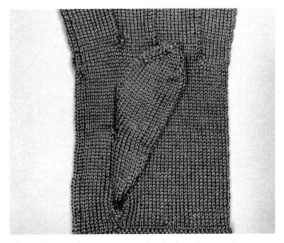

Thumb on palm, asymmetrical, showing no increases.

The Construction of the Thumb

How the thumb is shaped and constructed also varies, some methods increasing in the hand to form extra space for the thumb by means of a thumb gusset, or by making a slit in the fabric through which the thumb will fit.

A **symmetrical gusset thumb** works the increases for the thumb gusset at both sides of it, forming a symmetrical shape.

A **symmetrical gusset thumb** that is placed to the palm side of the hand is used in many published patterns. It means that the right and left hands are different.

An **asymmetrical thumb** has all the increases on one side of the thumb gusset. It, too, can be placed at the side of the hand or on the palm.

A **peasant thumb** is the simplest, and is made by making a slit on the palm side of the hand, usually by knitting some stiches with spare yarn, and then returning to them, taking out the spare yarn and knitting the resulting loops into the thumb. It's simpler than it sounds! This method is used in Pattern 5: 'Boreal Inspired' (Chapter 3).

The following thumb constructions are used in the patterns in this book:

- Chapter 1: Pattern 1, 'Plain Inspired', has a symmetrical thumb gusset placed at the side of the hand.
- Chapter 2: Pattern 2, 'Inspired by History', has an asymmetrical thumb gusset placed on the palm of the hand.
- Chapter 3:
    Pattern 3, 'Inspired by Mary Allen', has a symmetrical gusset placed towards the palm of the hand.
    Pattern 4, 'Inspired by Alba', has a symmetrical thumb gusset placed at the side of the hand.
    Pattern 5, 'Boreal Inspiration', has a peasant thumb on the palm of the hand.
- Chapter 5: Pattern 6, 'Vintage Inspiration', has an asymmetrical gusset placed on the palm of the hand.

The variety of thumbs gives the knitter the opportunity of making different ones.

Note: For these thumbs, once the stitches are back on the needles from the thumb gusset or slit, the thumb itself is most often just a tube until the shaping for the tip is reached. Occasionally there might be a little decreasing at the base of the thumb to bring down the stitch count, and this is found in Pattern 1, 'Plain Inspired', in Chapter 1.

Direction of Knitting

In fact, gloves do not have to be knitted from the cuff edge upwards. There are examples of gloves being knitted from the fingertips downwards – for example, the glove that is known as the glove of St Adalbert, in the treasury of St Vitus Cathedral, Prague, from the fourteenth century, as documented by Sylvie Odstrčilová in her article in 'Piecework', and in the present day, when gloves knitted in Nepal have been shown to be knitted in this way.

Gloves can also be knitted sideways, and an example of such a glove is shown in Chapter 5. Elizabeth Zimmermann gives a pattern for gloves that are hand knitted sideways in garter stitch in *Knit One, Knit All*, her book of garter-stitch garments from 2011. Patterns were also written for gloves made sideways on a knitting machine in the 1950s. The main disadvantage of this way of constructing a glove is, of course, the amount of sewing up to be done, whether that is actually sewing seams up the fingers, or joining stitches by grafting them together (Kitchener stitch).

Knitting Gloves

Gloves are fascinating to knit. They can challenge experienced knitters and use specific techniques in their construction. A small project, taking a small amount of yarn, gloves can be knitted with yarn from a stash. Whether on double-pointed or circular needles, they pack up small and are portable.

For the knitter new to gloves, it is strongly recommended that a plain pair is knitted first, tempting though it might be to launch into a patterned pair from the later chapters in this book. There are several specific operations and techniques to be undertaken in constructing a glove, and these are easier to manage with one yarn, rather than two. Having knitted a plain pair, the knitter is then equipped to knit more complex patterns, as well as being more confident to make their own modifications and additions. Knitting a plain pair gives an opportunity to try out new yarns and needles, and to understand the process of construction. It also gives the knitter the opportunity to check the fit, whoever the gloves are for. And if they don't fit the intended recipient, another one can soon be found.

So, where to start? It's likely that most knitters will have everything that is needed to make a pair of gloves, so let's have a look at what this might be.

Yarns for Glove Knitting

Of course, gloves can be knitted in any type of fibre and yarn, and a selection is shown. Wool, cotton, silk or synthetic yarns can all be used, depending on what is wanted. The most esoteric fibre ever used to knit gloves might be the sea silk (made from the long, silky filaments from a type of clam) found in a pair of gloves made in Italy in the late nineteenth century: an example is in the collection of the Victoria & Albert Museum, London, accession number T.15-1926 (*see* Resources). High-tech fibres such as Kevlar are used to make protective gloves for people who use sharp equipment in their work, such as butchers or tree surgeons.

Each fibre has its own advantages and disadvantages, of course. Wool keeps hands warm, cotton has no warmth but is decorative, and silk looks wonderful, is warm and strong, but has no stretch. Other fibres, and all the synthetic yarns or mixes of these, could also be used, according to personal preference, availability and budget. So, let's look at some of these in turn.

Wool and Its Relations

Sheep's wool, alpaca, mohair, cashmere and blends of these are all suitable for gloves as they are warm and have varying amounts of stretch. Shown from left to right are various wools from a pure wool 5-ply, superwash Merino, a mohair/Wensleydale blend, mohair/silk blend, angora/wool, wool/baby camel, and wool/linen/yak: they are all animal-protein fibres, except for the linen. Sheep's wool can retain warmth even when wet and so is really second

Yarns from various fibres, left to right: *alpaca, cotton, cashmere, silk, synthetic, wool.*

A selection of wools, left to right: *pure wool 5-ply, Superwash Merino, mohair/Wensleydale blend, mohair/silk blend, angora/wool, wool/baby camel, wool/linen/yak.*

to none for gloves for proper outdoor wear, especially in wet and cold places such as Britain. Wool stays warm even when it has nearly 30 per cent by weight of water in it, and in fact a warming process is set in place as hydrogen bonds break down in the moisture. This accounts for the distinctive smell of wet wool.

Alpaca or its mixes wears well and is also warm. Cashmere would make very luxurious gloves, warm and soft, but might not wear so well. Mohair, confusingly from the angora goat, is not often found in the type of yarn fine enough for gloves, although as a blend it adds strength and lustre to a sheep's wool. Angora, from the rabbit, might be used for cuffs but could be unsuitable for the whole glove because of the fluff and surplus fibres it produces. Camel and yak fibre can be found in blends with wools and silks to make interesting yarns from specialist suppliers: some examples are illustrated.

But especially if this is going to be a first pair of gloves, and if they are wanted for warmth, then sheep's wool is probably the fibre of first choice. There are many types of wool and thicknesses, but how it feels (its 'handle') and how it wears are going to be big factors in deciding what to use. So, if the gloves can be 'kept for best', then something soft and expensive might work, such as cashmere or even qiviut, the rare and very expensive fibre from the muskox. If just a single skein is needed this might be the project for some indulgence.

Merino and lambswool are soft, but, like cashmere, don't wear especially well. There are pure wools from British sheep that stand up to wear better, and one of these may be a good choice.

Sheep Breeds

The British Isles has many breeds of sheep, many of which have their own recognizable fleece and wool. The study of these is the stuff of a book in its own right. Using a pure wool breed yarn can be satisfying and is completely possible with so much of this type of yarn being produced in both the UK and around the world. Most of these pure-breed wools are produced by the artisan yarn sector, who, with access to mini mill spinning, can make yarns that are specific to their flocks. In a mini mill the processing can be managed so that the fibre from a particular flock can be processed on its own, enabling it to be identified as coming from a particular source. The availability of facilities such as this is obviously crucial for the existence of a specialist yarn industry.

The wool fairs that are held in the UK and elsewhere are good places to find these yarns, sometimes being shown with the animals that supplied the fibre. Or they might be bought when visiting a flock or farm, in which case gloves knitted from the yarn would make a nice souvenir.

Blends and Mixtures

This control over the fibre content of yarn means that innovative blends of different wools and fibres can be made, giving the contemporary knitter a huge variety of yarns. Some small batch yarns may use wool from two, three or

Pure sheep-breed wools, left to right: *Blue-Faced Leicester, dyed Gotland, dyed Jacob, dyed Rambouillet, natural Shetland, dyed Wensleydale.*

Artisan yarns, left to right: *100 per cent wool, hand-dyed Merino wool, organic pure wool, hand-dyed sock yarn (75 per cent wool, 25 per cent polyamide).*

four different breeds to capture the handle or colour of each wool. This of course makes a very individual and special yarn. Many blends combine a synthetic, usually polyamide (nylon), with wool to produce a hard-wearing yarn. The 75 per cent wool with 25 per cent polyamide blend in a 4-ply or fingering weight is a classic sock wool and one that would be entirely suitable for gloves. Such yarns are very often dyed so that they make stripes and patterns as they are knitted. Self-striping yarns can be fun to knit, and will cover any irregularities in a first pair of gloves! An example is illustrated in Chapter 4.

Yarn that is artisan dyed in small batches is also a good possibility for a pair of gloves, with the provisos outlined above about handle and wear. These are frequently dyed randomly or with pronounced colour variations, which could be attractive when knitted into gloves.

Hand-Spun Yarn

If you are a hand spinner, or are lucky enough to be given hand-spun wool yarn or to be able to buy it, then this can make lovely gloves. To be hard wearing it needs to be fairly firmly spun, but it will be very warm. A yarn with a slight unevenness in it can be attractive and will hide any lumps and bumps in the knitting too, as will yarns with a marl or a fleck in them. Gloves in hand-spun wool are fabulously cosy.

Vintage Yarns

Vintage yarns, mainly wools, can be extremely useful for glove knitting when a fine, strong, smooth yarn is required, in particular for gloves with small geometric patterns such as those found in Sanquhar gloves, discussed in Chapter 3. Fortunately these can be found in on-line sales sites and are usually not too expensive. Some are strengthened with a proportion of polyamide (nylon) as they were intended for sock knitting; this makes them ideal for gloves, an example being the Regia on the left of the illustration.

Type of Yarn and How it is Spun

A further consideration when choosing a yarn for knitting gloves is the spin of the yarn – that is, is it woollen spun or worsted spun? In the illustration the woollen spun yarn is on the left, while the worsted is on the right. This distinction can apply to yarns of any fibre, as it depends on how the fibres are treated prior to spinning. Basically, if the yarn is soft and quite open, with the fibres separated from each other, it is woollen spun; if it is smooth and not fluffy, with the fibres lying closer and parallel to each other, it is worsted spun. This is not a technical description, by the way! Some of the glove patterns that come later in this book use woollen-spun yarns, while in others, where a crisper definition of the stitch pattern is wanted, a smoother, pure wool, worsted spun yarn is more suitable.

Woollen and worsted spun yarns, left: *woollen spun*; right: *worsted spun.*

Vintage yarns, left to right: *Regia 3-ply (75 per cent wool, 25 per cent polyamide), Jaeger 3-ply pure wool, Patons Purple Heather, wool.*

Finding Out More about Wool and Woollen and Worsted Spinning

There is a lot of information about yarn production on the internet. The Blacker Yarn Company has information about fibre and spinning:
https://www.blackeryarns.co.uk/advice-information/all-about-yarn/
and the Brooklyn Tweed pages about woollen and worsted spinning are also informative:
https://brooklyntweed.com/pages/woolen-and-worsted-yarn
The videos of yarn production are especially fascinating!

Needles for Knitting Gloves

Gloves, when made by hand, are best knitted in the round. Knitting gloves flat entails a lot of seaming up the hands and for each finger and thumb. The patterns in this book are constructed in the round and are small enough projects to be a starter project if this has not been done before. For those who insist on knitting gloves on two needles there are patterns out there on the internet! For circular knitting a variety of knitting needles can be used.

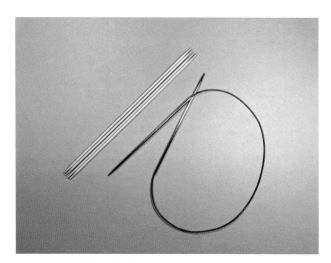
Knitting needles suitable for knitting gloves.

Double-Pointed Needles (dpns)

Until the knitting revival of the twenty-first century, double-pointed needles (dpns) were almost the only way to knit in the round, and they are still widely used by many knitters. Double-pointed needles have the advantage of being relatively cheap to buy, and many knitters have a selection passed on from older family members. The image shows dpns in aluminium, carbon fibre, bamboo, wood and steel, left to right. Vintage double-pointed needles are most often metal, coated aluminium or steel, and sometimes plastic. More recently, however, they have been produced in wood, bamboo or carbon fibre. If you like to knit with double-pointed needles you are spoilt for choice. Bamboo needles are good for a beginner knitter in the round as the finish is not too smooth and the yarn has some grip on their surface. They are also light and so tend to stay in place (not tending to slide out of the stitches) better than heavier metal needles.

Look at the ends of the needles: are they pointed or blunt? Given the option, for gloves, choose pointed ones every time to give the precision for picking up stitches and other operations while knitting gloves.

As for length, that is personal choice. For a 'put the needle under the arm' knitter, then the longest double-pointed needles would clearly suit, although they are perhaps a bit unwieldy for a small item such as a glove. Long – that is, 34cm (13.5in) – dpns are available on the internet.

If buying new double-pointed needles, they are usually available in 20cm (8in), 15cm (6in) and 10cm (4in) lengths. The longer length gives more flexible use for larger projects such as hats, while the shorter ones are more convenient for the fingers and thumbs of gloves.

How many needles to use?

Double-pointed needles are sold in sets of four or five, and how many are used is a personal choice. The stitches can be on two needles and knitted with the third, as is done in Shetland. This is an acquired skill, however, and unless there is a particular reason to do it this way, it is more comfortable with the stitches on three needles and knitting with the fourth, as is common in the UK, as shown. If using the set of five, the stitches are on four needles and the knitting is done with the fifth, as illustrated. This method is more common in the Baltic countries and Scandinavia.

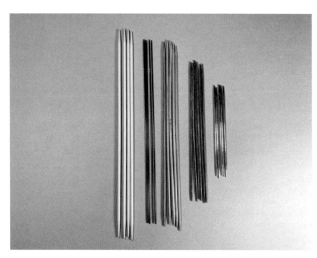
Double-pointed needles, old and new.

Glove ribbing being knitted with four double-pointed needles.

An Estonian cuff being knitted with five double-pointed needles.

Vintage circular needles from the Knitting & Crochet Guild Collection. (Norman Taylor)

My personal preference is for a set of four, with the stitches divided on to three needles and knitting with the fourth. The triangular configuration makes the knitting and the needles stable. A set of five needles, with the knitting on four, makes it easier to divide the work up according to the pattern, and instructions written for this style of knitting will give stitch increases, for example, per needle. However, five needles can be tricky to control in the early stages of the work.

Circular Needles

Circular needles have been available for a surprising length of time. The earliest of those pictured, in the Knitting & Crochet Guild Collection, date perhaps from the 1930s, to judge from the pictures on the packets. However, circular needles are much more common and more widely used now, and are available in many types and lengths. This variety can be confusing, and circulars are expensive to buy, so it's good to have an idea of what you might prefer to use before a big investment.

Circular needles consist of the 'needle' part of the needle, one at each end, rigid and of a measured size, and the flexible cable that joins the two needles. The length of the rigid section varies with the length of the cable, so a 60cm (24in) has a rigid section of about 12cm (5in), while a 40cm (16in) circular has a rigid section of 8cm (3in). That difference in length affects how many stitches can fit, but also, and more importantly, how the needle sits in the hands. The materials for circular needles, needle part and cable part include metal,

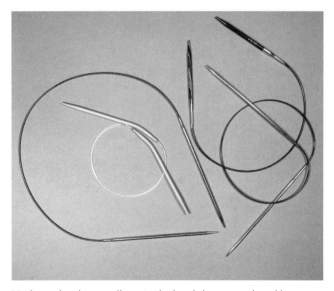

Various circular needles: steel, aluminium, wood and brass, all with plastic cables.

wood and plastic in many combinations. Add to this the variations in size of needle and length of cable, and there are many thousands of permutations.

Interchangeable Circular Needles

Circulars are also available as interchangeables, where a joining system allows for different size needles to be joined to

The Tools for the Job

Glove knitting is skilled work and demands a good, fine-pointed needle of any type to make manipulating stitches easier. Look out for 'lace' points when ordering or buying. Other features that may affect the choice are the finish of the needle and the colour of the cable. Stainless-steel needles are durable but often have a high polish on them, which can be hard on the eyes, especially under artificial light. Aluminium ones, being a matte light grey, are easier on the eyes, but the stitches do not move on them as well, especially over the joint between the needle and cable. Wood and bamboo hold the stitches better, having more friction than metals. So it really is a matter of the tools for the job.

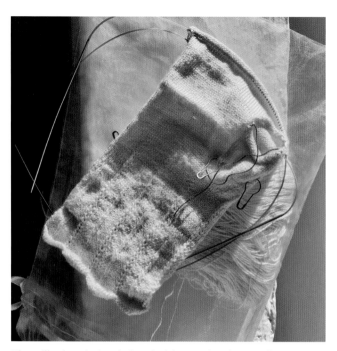

Fine silk glove being knitted with two circular needles.

different lengths of cable. The range of sizes is not comprehensive, however, and often doesn't include the finer sizes that may be wanted for glove knitting. There is a large range of these, in all materials, but the lowest needle size in the set is usually 3–3.5mm, so unless these are available it might not be worth buying a set with glove knitting in mind. There are strong opinions about this sort of needle – it would be sensible to ask around for people's preferences before buying, as they are quite an outlay. Also, new sorts are coming on to the market all the time.

Knitting with Two Circular Needles

Fine silk is shown being knitted on two circular needles in the image. Knitting in the round on two circular needles is also shown in the process pictures, and is my favourite method. The stitches are secure, and the work divides into the front and back of the hand, with one section on each needle.

In this system the stitches are divided between both needles, roughly in half, but this is not crucial. The stitches are pushed up to the end of the needle in the left hand, assuming you knit right-handed, and the opposite end of the needle the stitches are on is taken by the right hand and the stitches knitted off on to that. It doesn't make a lot of sense until it is tried. After that, people either love it or loathe it.

Magic Loop with a Single Circular Needle

The magic loop system enables the knitter to make use of one long circular needle to knit in the round. It can be useful for knitting the fingers of gloves. The photo shows the stitches being knitted from one end of the needle to the other on the cuff of a glove in a tweedy wool.

Magic loop method used for the cuff and wrist of a wool glove.

Just One Other Type of Needle...

Flexible double-pointed needles, short in length and sold in sets of three, are a relatively recent addition to the tools available for knitting in the round. A set is shown in the illustration, and the brown and charcoal cuff is being knitted on them. These must be tried for the knitter to know if they like them or not. They are not cheap, so if some can be borrowed for a test run that would be good before committing to buying a set or sets.

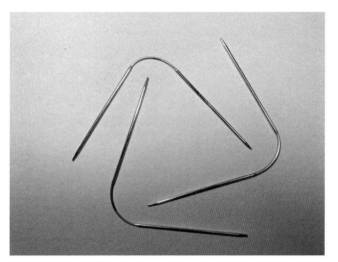

A set of three flexible double-pointed needles.

Knitting on three short needles.

A combination of all these types of needle – double-pointed, circulars, used singly or in pairs – might be tried when starting out on glove knitting. One set of tools might work well for, say, the hand, but another for the fingers. There are no hard and fast rules – the knitter can choose.

Other Tools Needed

Needle Gauge

A needle gauge is an essential piece of kit for knitters using double-pointed and circular needles. Even if these are kept

Avoiding 'Second Glove Syndrome'

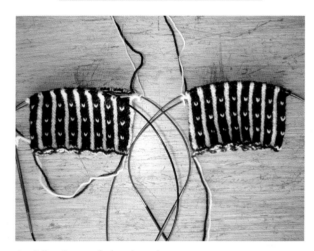

Avoiding 'second glove' syndrome.

With items such as socks and gloves, where two of the same type have to be knitted, many makers struggle with making the second one. This can be avoided by having both gloves on the go at the same time. Each glove is knitted separately, each part being done in turn; that is, cast on one, cast on the other, knit the cuff of the first one, knit the cuff of the second. In this way it is possible to keep track of exactly how things have been done, while any modifications are fresh in the mind. The only disadvantage here is that if knitting on two circulars, to avoid a lot of transferring from one set to another, four of the same size have to be bought, which can be costly.

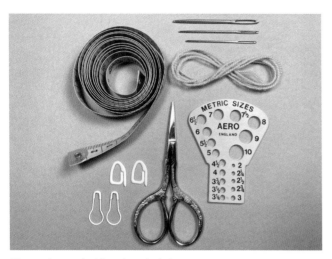
The tools needed for glove knitting.

in their packets, or in marked cases, they will escape and become an unknown quantity. One fine grey aluminium double-pointed needle can look very similar to another, even if they are different sizes. Some manufacturers try to mark these types of needle, but with limited success. Needle gauges come in combination with rulers, yarn holders and various other gadgets, and can be mass produced, artisanal, new or vintage, so there's plenty of choice. Have several! Also, make sure that they are labelled with all the systems of sizing needles – millimetres, old UK sizes and US sizes. Most gauges, apart from some vintage ones, only go down to a 2mm needle measurement, in which case the packaging on the needles has to be relied on for needles any smaller than this.

Sewing-Up Needles

Most knitters will have these needles in a variety of sizes. With both blunt tip and large eye, these will be needed for placing saved stitches on to lengths of thread. They will also be needed for darning in the ends and tidying up any gaps at the base of the fingers.

Lengths of Thread

Lengths of thread are for saving stitches. Scrap yarn is fine, but make sure it is strong and smooth. It also needs to be a good contrast colour to the yarn being knitted, and of a similar thickness. Avoid anything at all fluffy or hairy otherwise the fibres will mark where the stitches were held for ever! Stitch holders could be used but they can be too rigid and can get in the way of further knitting.

Stitch Markers

Stitch markers can be anything from a length of yarn made into a loop, calabash pins, mass-produced plastic, or very decorative bought ones. Safety pins and paperclips are not recommended but might do in an emergency. Stitch markers are essential in the early part of knitting a glove, for marking the increases for the thumb gusset on a plain glove, and for marking where patterns will fall. The choice of what sort to use is completely personal. Despite what many patterns say, a stitch marker is not necessary to mark the start of a round – the end of the cast-on yarn will do that job.

What to Keep it All in?

There is the most fabulous choice of knitting bags on the market and many yarn shops and suppliers give away cloth bags with their yarn. For me, clear plastic bags cannot be beaten for the fact that the work can be seen instantly. Their negative environmental implications are obvious, however, and I reuse them *ad infinitum* to reduce their impact!

Making Notes

It's essential to keep track of glove knitting. There's a lot going on most of the time, so a notebook and pencil is essential, or the note-taking app on a phone or tablet. You can never write down too much about knitting a glove, especially if one is being knitted before the other, rather than both together.

Decorative stitch markers made with upcycled beads and buttons. (Credit: thiscraftyoctopus)

Knitting bags.

If you are going to work out colour patterns, then a pad of squared paper is useful. There are also templates on the internet for knitters to print out.

And Lastly...

On a personal note, I always have some hand cream alongside my knitting – gloves or non gloves. A tube or pot of something you like can help to grip the needles and yarn if hands get dry. It also gives an opportunity for a bit of a massage and stretch for the fingers and wrists.

And a bit of self-care…glove knitting can be concentrated work. Remember to get up and stretch your fingers, arms and shoulders at regular intervals. Use a task manager app on your phone to do this, or just a kitchen timer!

Techniques for Glove Knitting

Techniques have been discussed with respect to the various options for tools, but here are some additional notes. This is not intended to be exhaustive given the huge volume of help for knitters on the internet, especially via YouTube where professional videos are available from multiple providers. There are some pointers in the box later in this section.

If you do not use the internet, a good standard knitting reference book is useful, such as those of Mary Thomas or Montse Stanley (*see* Bibliography).

Techniques for Knitting Plain Gloves

Note: For a 'normal' glove, knitted upwards from the cuff, there is casting on at the start and then more to construct the thumb and fingers.

For techniques for knitting with more than one colour, *see* Chapter 3, Patterned Gloves in Yorkshire, Scotland and Estonia.

Casting on at the Cuff

In general, for the cuff, a long tail thumb cast-on is suitable for plain gloves. Any glove cast-on needs to be both stretchy and durable, and this is one that does the job. The first round can be knitted flat before joining into the round, which is especially useful when working in more than one colour.

Joining into the Round at the Cuff

If one extra stitch is cast on, that can be transferred on to the other needle after the cast-on. It is then knitted together on the first round to make a firm join.

Knitting in the Round

There are several ways of doing this, and each knitter will have an individual preference for which tools to use – double-pointed needles (dpns), circular needles used in pairs, a long circular needle used for magic loop, or a set of three short bendy needles. It's possible to use different techniques for various parts of the glove, depending on what needles are available. Cuffs and hands might be knitted on dpns, while magic loop with a single long circular needle can work for fingers.

Increasing in the Round

The most often used increases are the M1L and M1R, in which the loop between two stitches is lifted, put on to the left-hand needle and knitted into. Full instructions are given in the Abbreviations list at the back of the book.

Taking Stitches off Needles and on to Threads

Use a blunt-pointed wool needle for this, and a length of smooth, strong yarn in a contrasting colour to the knitting. The yarn should be of a similar weight to the knitting as this makes handling the stitches easier later in the process.

Casting on for Finger and Thumb Constructions: Various Ways

To construct the fingers and thumb, stitches have to be cast on. This can be done in several ways. In all of them, the work has to be turned before the cast-on is started.

1. The **two-needle cast-on** is worked with both needles by knitting a stitch and placing it on the left-hand needle. The loops of this cast-on can be big, so it's good to tighten them by knitting into the backs on the next round.
2. In the **backward loop cast-on**, loops are made on the left-hand needle by twisting the knitting yarn and placing it on the left-hand needle. This cast-on is tricky to manage as it can both tighten or loosen, giving long strands between stitches. I do not recommend it.
3. The **purl cable cast-on** is worked by purling into the gap between the stitches on the left-hand needle and placing the resulting stitch on the needle. This produces the neatest result.

Joining Back into the Round

This is where another pair of hands would be useful! The stitches to be joined to form a finger or thumb should be held as close together as possible when the first round is knitted on them. If a gap appears it can be neatened after the glove is finished using a needle and the yarn left at the start of the finger or thumb.

Pick up and Knit

Ideally, for an almost invisible join between the stitches of one finger and the other, a pick-up is done into each stitch. For example, if four stitches were cast on, then four will be picked up. This is not always possible, however, as sometimes the pattern has to allow for extra stitches so that the fingers can be the right size, in which case some fudging has to take place. The neatest pick-up is obtained by going down into the fabric with the tip of the needle and bringing the yarn up as cleanly as possible between the existing stitches. A crochet hook can be used to bring the yarn through ready to be knitted. This works the same for any picking up on cardigan edges or neck bands.

Shaping Fingertips and Finishing

Usually, patterns give instructions for how the shaping at the fingertip should be done. This can be paired decreases, or decreases spaced around the finger as appropriate. Decreases worked at intervals in the same direction give a spiral shape to the fingertip.

Finishing off the fingertip is done by breaking the yarn and using a wool needle, threading it through the remaining stitches. In her book *Estonian Knitting*, Nancy Bush calls this 'Heart of a blossom', translated from the Estonian for the process.

Note: A neater effect can be achieved by pulling the stitches tighter while they are on the needles, before threading the yarn through them.

Sewing in the Ends and Neatening the Work

Darning in the ends of the yarn can be used as an opportunity to neaten any gaps or irregularities that might have appeared at the base of the fingers. Leave plenty of yarn when rejoining for the fingers and thumb for this purpose.

Pressing, Blocking and Washing

For wool, use a hot iron and damp cloth and hover the iron over the glove fabric to steam it lightly. Blocking can be done by pinning the glove out. An ironing board is the ideal place for this.

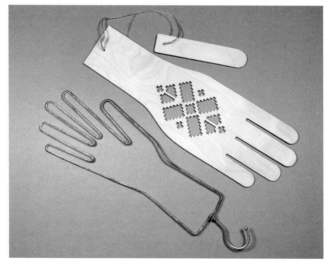

Glove blockers: vintage and modern from the KCG Collection.

Glove blockers are available at differing prices. The illustration shows a vintage wire blocker from the Collection of the Knitting & Crochet Guild, and a contemporary version imported from Estonia – one of each pair. It's also possible to improvise with home-made ones – instructions for making them are on the internet (*see* Resources at the back of this book).

Some wools, especially the artisan-type ones and pure breeds, which can be quite springy, benefit from a gentle wash after completion. Squeeze the gloves gently in a drop of sudsy water (lots of choice of what to use here, from washing-up liquid to specialist wool and hand-wash liquid, or a drop of shower gel or shampoo!). Then roll them up in a clean dry towel and squeeze or twist hard. Unroll the towel, retrieve the gloves, pat them out and place them somewhere warm to dry. For other fibres, follow the instructions with the yarn.

Be warned: silk can stretch in washing. For finishing just a light steam is best.

Considering the Finished Size, or Does Size Matter?

Like any other knitted garment, the size of gloves depends on several things: the number of stitches, the size of the needle, and the thickness of the yarn used. The patterns in this book have been designed to produce gloves in a range of sizes. As with all knitted garments, the resultant size is dependent on the tension or gauge at which the knitting is produced. If knitted to that specified in the patterns, the gloves will turn out in the size indicated. But if this is not the case, size will vary.

There are various ways of managing size, the first being to check the tension of knitting. Bear in mind that this might vary depending on the method of knitting. In the round and flat, fabrics will almost certainly have different stitch counts from each other. The type of needles being used will also affect stitch counts. This is discussed more in Chapter 4, where calculating the stitches for individual designs is covered. Secondly, as long as the gloves are not being kept a secret from the person who will wear them, they can be tried on at any stage of the making. If using circular needles, this can be done with them in place; for knitting that is on double-pointed needles, it's probably safer to put the partly knitted work on a length of spare yarn – strong and smooth, of course.

Remember that knitting is stretchy, especially if wool is used, and some variation in size is perhaps forgivable.

Resources for Glove Knitting on the Internet

The internet is a rich source of guidance and help for knitters, and glove knitters are well provided for here. These are just a few starting points, with the obvious proviso that they may not all be current over the lifespan of a printed book.

Patterns
There are many free patterns for gloves on the internet, mainly on the knitters' site, Ravelry. These can be found by searching the pattern database under 'Accessories' and then going on to the type of gloves required.

Materials: Yarns and Tools
Again, many of the specialist yarns and tools that might be wanted for knitting gloves – fine circular needles, for example – are readily available on-line. Of course, if you have a favourite knitting shop in real life, then do use it!

Techniques
A site called Very Pink Knits has an excellent video that takes the viewer through the process of knitting a glove (*see* Resources at the back of this book).

Other techniques that are needed when knitting gloves are also in videos on the internet, including:

· Knitting in the round on double-pointed needles
· Knitting in the round on two circulars
· Knitting in the round using the magic loop method
· Casting on for the thumb and fingers – various methods: purl cable cast-on is recommended. This is often found as an instruction for making the underarm stitches in top-down garments rather than for glove construction: *see* titles such as 'avoiding underarm holes in top-down sweaters'
· M1L and M1R for paired increases for the thumb shaping
· Casting on with two colours of yarn
· Knitting with two colours of yarn

All these are covered by many knitters on YouTube. Browse through to find one whose style you like and whose instructions you find clear and useful. My personal favourite is Very Pink Knits.

The Process of Knitting a Glove

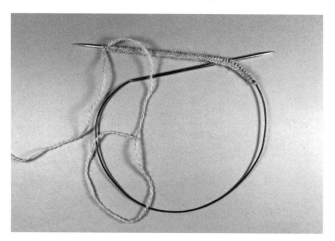

Stitches cast on, one needle.

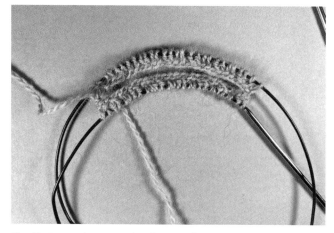

The first round on two circular needles.

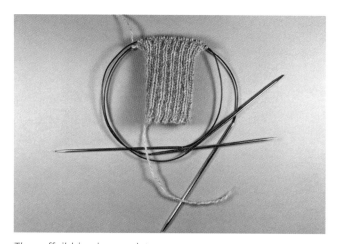

The cuff ribbing is complete.

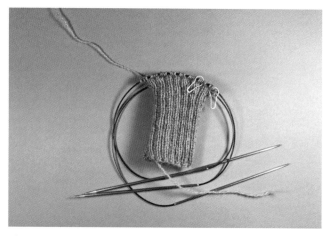

Thumb gusset started and marked.

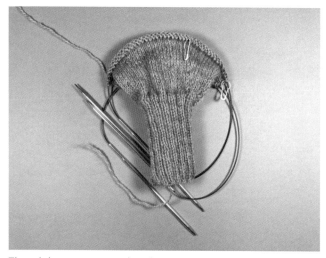

Thumb increases completed.

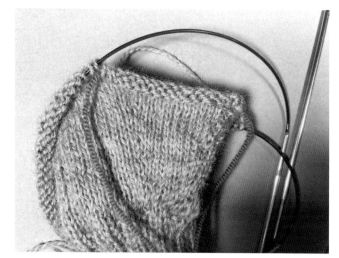

Thumb stitches in close-up.

Cast-on stitches above the thumb.

Hand knitted to the base of the fourth finger.

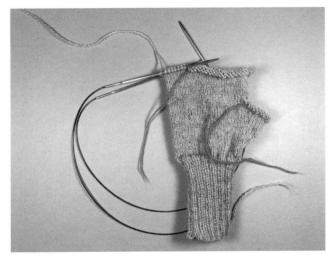

Fourth-finger stitches on needles.

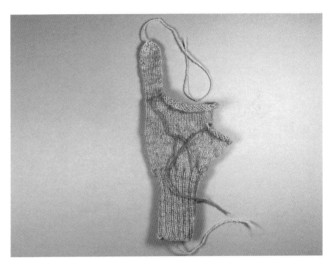

Fourth finger completed.

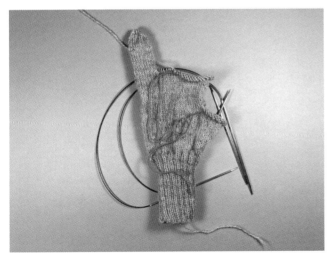

Third-finger stitches on needles after hand extension.

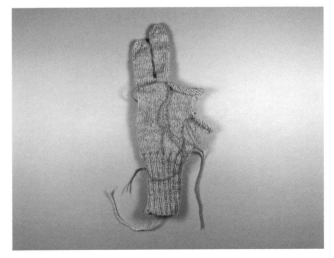

Third finger complete.

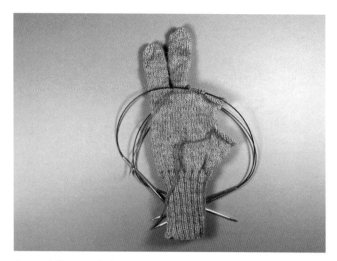

Second-finger stitches on needles.

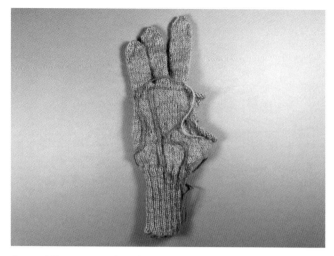

Second finger completed.

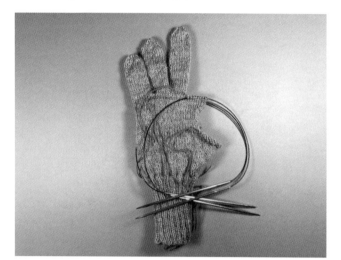

First-finger stitches on needles.

First finger completed.

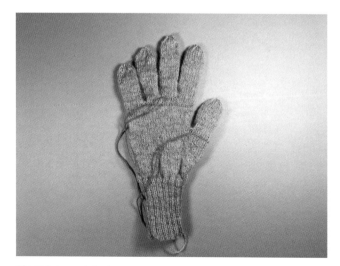

Thumb completed.

The ends darned in.

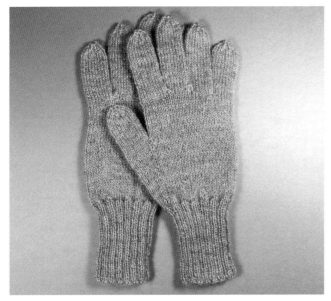

After a wash and light press.

The sequence of events in the knitting of a glove can be seen in the process pictures provided here. These show the plain glove being knitted, but this could be easily altered by the addition of, say, stripes in the cuff or hand, or different colours for the fingers. Chapter 4 discusses further ways of adding features and variations.

The pair illustrated was knitted on two circular needles, but other methods would give the same finished product.

Before You Start – Some Handy Hints for Glove Knitters

- Use the method of knitting in the round that you prefer – experiment with different ones.
- Use the longest needle you can – your hands will thank you for it. Bear in mind that longer circular needles have a longer straight section of needle to hold and knit on.
- Cast on keeping the knitting flat, knit one row, then join the work into the round and continue knitting.
- You may want to knit the rib on a finer needle than the hand. This gives a snugger cuff but is not essential. Patterns vary as to whether this is specified.
- Make one extra stitch in the cast-on, and then knit that and the first stitch from the round to make a secure join for the round.
- Use the end of the yarn from casting on as a marker for the start of the round; there is no need for a stitch marker.
- Do use stitch markers for the placing of the thumb gusset shaping – a length of spare yarn will do, tied into a loop. Make sure it is smooth, strong and non-fluffy, and a contrast to the working yarn.
- When picking up stitches and casting on at the base of fingers: add extra stitches at the base of the fingers, say one at each end of the cast-on or pick up and knit, then knit two together to correct the stitch count on the next round. This helps to close holes at the base of the fingers.
- Push the completed fingers into the hand when knitting the next ones. This gets them out of the way.
- Take out the scrap or holding thread once the stitches have been knitted on plain gloves. The thread can distort the stitches, and this can be hard to get rid of. Pop in a stitch marker to mark the start of the finger rows.
- Make sure you are in good light, either by a window or with a good worklamp or even a head torch.
- Get up and stretch and move around at regular intervals – use a work management app that gives, say, twenty-five-minute blocks with five-minute breaks. Glove knitting is hard work, and the knitter needs a break!
- Mistakes: It depends on the type of mistake as to whether or not you need to unpick the work to correct it. A stitch or two out on the finger of a fine plain glove won't matter, but a mistake in colourwork initials will! The latter can be corrected using Swiss darning (duplicate stitch) without detection.

Pattern 1: Plain Inspired

This pattern for a pair of plain gloves is a good starting point for a beginner glove knitter. The pattern specifies a yarn that has a lot of life, but other similar weight yarns could be substituted. Check the length per weight before going ahead though! Note that the right and left gloves are the same as the thumb is placed on the side of the hand. If the amount of yarn is an issue, then knit the ribbing shorter, 4cm/1.5in, instead of 7cm/2.75in.

Materials

Yarn

Blacker Yarns, Tamar Lustre Blend 4-ply, 100% British wool, 100g skein, 350m/380 yds/100g, colour Tiddy Brook lemon green, 1 skein.
Finished gloves weigh 56g and take 195m/209 yds approx.

Needles

3 mm knitting needles or size to achieve gauge (*see* Chapter 1 for type of knitting needles).
2.75mm needles for the rib, if preferred but not essential.

Pattern 1: 'Plain Inspired Gloves'.

Tools

Stitch markers or lengths of contrasting yarn tied into loops. Stitch holders and/or lengths of smooth strong contrasting yarn for holding stitches.
Wool sewing needle and scissors for finishing.

Finished size:
To fit a medium adult hand.
Length: 28cm/11in.
All round above thumb: 18cm/7in.

Tension/gauge:
30 sts x 38 rounds = 10cm/4in square over stocking stitch knitted in the round.

Abbreviations:
See abbreviations list at back of book

Special techniques:
See 'Techniques for knitting plain gloves' in Chapter 1, which covers 'casting on for finger and thumb constructions: various ways'.

Instructions

Note: both gloves are the same.

Cuff
CO 56 sts on 3mm (or 2.75mm if preferred) needles. Join for working in the round.
PM for start of round if wanted, checking sts are not twisted.
Work in K2 P2 rib for 7cm/2.75in OR 4cm/1.5in for short cuff version.
Change to 3mm needles if necessary. K1 round.

Start shaping thumb gusset:
Set up round: K27 sts, PM, M1R, K2, M1L, PM. K 27 to end of round. 2 sts inc; 58 sts.
Step 1: K 3 rounds.
Step 2: K to marker, SLM, M1R, K4, M1L, SLM. 2 sts inc; 60 sts.
Work Steps 1 and 2 for a total of 7 times. 14 sts inc; 72 sts.

Make the thumb opening:

K27 sts, place 18 sts between the markers onto a length of contrast yarn, CO 4 sts, K 27 to end of round; 58 sts

Above the thumb:

Knit for 5cm/2in or length required, on these 58 sts from thumb gusset cast-on.

Work the fingers

Fourth finger:

K8 sts, put 42 sts onto a length of contrast yarn, CO 2 sts, K last 8 sts; 18 sts. Working in the round, knit until finger measures 6cm/2.5in, or length required.

Shape the tip:

Next round: K1, K2tog 6 times; 12 sts.
Next round: K
Next round: K2tog 6 times; 6 sts.
Cut yarn, draw through sts, tighten and fasten off.

Extend hand:

Return to sts on contrast yarn, re-join yarn, knit all round 42 sts, PUK 2 sts from base of fourth finger; 44 sts total.
K2 rounds.

Third finger:

K7 sts, put 28 sts on to contrast yarn, CO 2 sts, K last 7 sts on contrast yarn, PUK 2 from base of fourth finger, 18 sts. Working in the round, knit until finger measures 7.5cm/3in or length required.
Finish tip as for little finger.

Second finger:

Return to sts on contrast yarn, K 7 sts, CO 2 sts, K last 7 sts on contrast yarn, PUK 2 sts from base of third finger, 18 sts. Working in the round knit for 8.5cm/3.25in or length required.
Finish tip as for little finger.

First finger:

K 14 sts left on contrast yarn, PUK 4 sts from base of second finger, 18 sts.
Knit 7.5cm/3in or until length required.
Finish tip as for little finger.

Knit the thumb:

Return to sts on contrast yarn for thumb gusset, K18, PUK 4 sts from thumb gusset CO, 22 sts.
K 6 rounds.

Shape thumb:

Next round: K18, K2tog tbl, K2tog. 2 sts dec; 20 sts.
Knit until thumb measures 5cm/2in or length required.

Shape the tip:

Next round: K1, K2tog 6 times, K2; 14 sts.
Next round: K
Next round: K2tog 7 times; 7 sts.
Cut yarn, draw through sts, tighten and fasten off.

Knit the second glove to match. As the gloves are symmetrical there is not a right and a left glove although this preference will become apparent in wear.

Finishing:

Darn in all ends, closing any gaps at the base of the fingers as necessary. Give the gloves a light press with a hot iron and damp cloth or according to instructions given with the yarn.

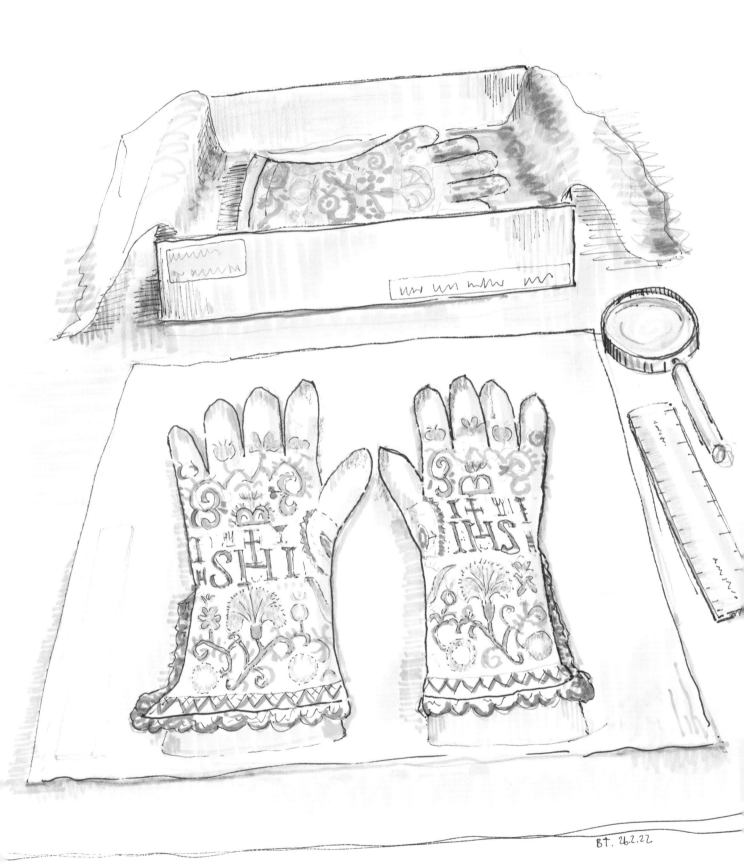

BT. 26.2.22

CHAPTER 2

A HISTORY OF KNITTING OR A HISTORY OF KNITTED GLOVES?

Gloves as a Form of Clothing

The glove form requires a certain sophistication and ability to manipulate materials, whether these are fabrics, leathers or yarns. Like every type of artefact made by people, gloves and other hand coverings come in a huge range of forms, as was shown in Chapter 1. Those that have survived to provide us with material evidence in the present day are most likely to be those that were precious and made for important people. The history of the glove form will never be told with complete accuracy as the material evidence is very flimsy before the twelfth century: there are not that many gloves surviving from thousands of years ago.

However, one glove that has come down the millennia was in the tomb of Tutankhamun, the Egyptian king, discovered when it was famously opened in 1923 by the British archaeologist Howard Carter. This glove is thought to be the earliest example of the form, and dates back at least 3,000 years. It has four fingers and a thumb, and is constructed from two sorts of woven fabric, both linen. As in so many aspects of life, the ancient Egyptians had the skills to make sophisticated artefacts, fingered gloves among them.

Tantalizingly for any trace of gloves before this one, the evidence is a tiny drawing on a piece of bone that was first seen and noted and identified as a glove form by the archaeologist and scientist, W.G. Dawkins, in late Victorian times. This glove form seems to reach up the arm of its wearer and has at least three fingers, in some sort of arrangement that would allow the fingers to move. Dawkins assumes it was made from animal skins. So this seems to be evidence that the glove form has been in existence since people lived in caves and had the means and ability to draw.

It can be conjectured, from brief references in records, that people fashioned protection for the hands when performing a variety of tasks in agriculture or construction, as well as hunting and archery. Gloves are referred to in writings of the Ancient Greeks, Homer noting that they were worn by Laertes, the father of Odysseus, to cut back thorns while gardening. The Romans also knew of the glove form with fingers, as it is mentioned by Virgil and other writers, gloves with fingers having a particular name: *digitalia*.

Surviving gloves from the past are found made of leather and various animal skins, fabric, and sometimes metallic elements. These materials do not often survive the passage of time, so what is known about them is subject to their remains being identified as parts of hand coverings. This is often not certain, especially when looking at fragments of artefacts from more than several centuries ago that may be so damaged as to be unrecognizable.

However, the knitted glove has yet to appear as part of textile history. As with so much costume history, it is the garments that belonged to the rich and powerful that come down to us in collections now. Gloves that belonged to royalty and those used in coronations are represented, and almost all of these were made of leather or skins of various sorts. It is likely that there were many rough gloves or hand coverings used through the centuries that were just worn out or discarded, and being natural materials, either skin or fabric, rotted away to nothing. Those gloves that were made for royalty or the church tend to be the ones that have been kept for posterity.

Evidence exists, both material and documentary, for the use of gloves in the Christian Church from about the tenth century onwards. These gloves are described as being made of linen, possibly from pieced cloth, and always white to denote purity. Linen, rather than leather, was insisted upon by religious authorities, as leather was considered to be 'too carnal' for such close contact with the skin, according to Gwen Emlyn-Jones in her 1970s book, *Glove Making: The Art and the Craft*. She says this was the case for any religious ministration, whether that of the Egyptian Pharoah or the English bishop.

Some of the earliest gloves still in existence were made from linen in a knotting technique, in which the threads are formed into a fabric using a needle, often known by its Norwegian name of *nalbinding*. The history of knitting can be said to start here, in the development of a fabric structure that did not require a sewing needle to make it, and is a development from *nalbinding*.

Introduction to the History of Knitting

The history of knitting has often been portrayed inaccurately. Knitting has erroneously been said to date from ancient times and to be associated with great antiquity. Myths and legends have been constructed without authentication based on material evidence, and these often involve ancient history, biblical and mythical figures, with a fair amount of death and associated bodies. These tales have become popular and are often repeated! In fact, based on the material evidence, knitting is now known to be a relatively recent technique, dating from perhaps about the eleventh to twelfth centuries CE (Common Era). So rather than repeating all the inaccurate and misleading, albeit attractive, stories about the antiquity of knitting, let's have a look at what is actually known about it. Like a proper detective, the true historian of knitting bases their conclusions on real evidence. Gloves are a good 'vehicle' for this, for several reasons, as will be seen.

Because gloves were often such special and highly valued articles, they are a good way to look at history, having frequently survived through various means, and against the odds. Being small, they can be kept and stored relatively easily. Some, being valuable, have been kept in collections or buried with their owners as part of ceremonial dress. This chapter looks at those knitted gloves that have survived for whatever reasons through the centuries, taking a chronological approach from the earliest known knitted gloves to the end of the nineteenth century. The more recent history of gloves, from the turn of the twentieth century, will be picked up in the next chapter, Chapter 3.

The glove of Pierre de Courpalay made from looping. (Photo © RMN-Grand Palais (Musée de Cluny – Musée National du Moyen Âge)/Jean-Gilles Berizzi)

The Emergence of 'True' Knitting through Gloves

Gloves for high-ranking clergy exist because, from about the tenth century onwards, the Pope, bishops and other important members of the Catholic clergy wore them for a part of services or mass. As mentioned earlier, some of these may have been pieced from linen fabric, but others pre-date the introduction of knitting to Europe and were made from looping techniques, or *nalbinding*. Very few of these liturgical gloves made from non-knitting techniques have survived, although a small number still exist in European museums and cathedrals.

These looping methods, which are extremely laborious, produce a variety of fabrics that can look similar to lace, crochet or knitting. However, they are none of these. These fabrics were made using a thread and needle, with the thread being guided through the previous loop with the needle, unlike knitting, in which the thread is just pulled partly through the loop by the needle. A very fine example of the technique from France, sadly in very poor condition, is shown. This glove, made from fine silk, belonged to Pierre de Courpalay, a French bishop who died in 1334.

Once knitting became known in Europe, perhaps having been brought from the area which is now Syria, across North Africa and into Italy and Spain, liturgical gloves became one of the first types of item to be made from true knitting. This may be because it would have been much easier to construct a fine glove using knitting as the technique, rather than *nalbinding* or knotting. Perhaps skilled workers would have been keen to show their prowess by making these high-status artefacts using the latest and improved methods? Their making was very likely associated with Muslim craft workers or *mudejar* knitters, who were working for the Christian church. However, it must be emphasized that this is conjecture, and no material evidence exists to support these ideas.

Liturgical Gloves – their Survival

Although no accurate dating has been carried out, gloves for religious use (properly known as *liturgical* gloves, but also as ecclesiastical, bishop's or pontifical gloves) were made from a true knitted fabric from the twelfth century onwards. The early knitted examples are plain white silk. The decoration is applied in the form of a metallic or embroidered medallion on the back of each hand. Most were made from silk, or very

Knitted silk gloves in the basilica of Saint Sernin, Toulouse.

occasionally linen or cotton, because using leather or animal skin was not considered appropriate, being too closely related to the body.

An example of silk knitted gloves, shown in the drawing, is the pair on display in the treasury of the basilica of Saint Sernin, in Toulouse, southern France. These might be the earliest example of true knitting in existence, according to Dominique Cardon, who studied these and other liturgical gloves in the 1990s, the findings from which are reported in an article in French (*see* Bibliography). The lower edge was decorated with a narrow braid that has mostly vanished, as these are in a poor state of repair. What remains of the gloves is supported on a finer fabric for conservation purposes. They are dated by the techniques used in the manufacture of the copper plaques on their backs, which are from the twelfth century, although of course this date may not be that of the knitted fabric. They are often known as the gloves of Saint Remi, a saint said to have lived many centuries earlier, well before the gloves.

A similar pair, in better condition, as shown in the photo, is to be found as part of the cathedral treasure in Brixen or Bressanone, in the north of Italy, now kept in the Hofburg

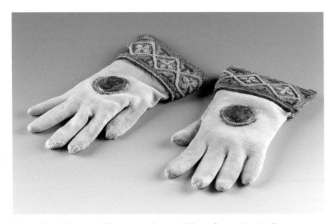
Liturgical gloves with enamel medallions from the Hofburg Museum, Brixen (Bressanone), Italy. (© Hofburg Brixen Bressanone)

Liturgical gloves are also found in museums, such as the Brixen gloves, which have been transferred from church treasuries. In other cases they have often entered museums through donations from private collections, and nothing is known of their history.

The Characteristics of these Gloves

The surviving liturgical gloves are finely worked, whether the basic glove is plain and then decorated with embroidery or metallic roundels, or the fabric of the glove itself has patterns and ornamentation worked in. There is often further ornamentation in either case, with braids or laces around the cuff, or tassels attached at the lower edges. One of the most highly ornamented pairs ever found, which has patterns all over and bobbin lace around the fingers and thumb, is in the collection of the Victoria & Albert Museum, London; it is available to be seen through the on-line catalogue (accession number 437&A-1892) – *see* the Resources section at the back of the book.

The gloves held in the cathedral of St Bertrand de Comminges, in the south-west of France, are a lovely example of liturgical gloves in which the patterns are knitted into the fabric. The illustration shows them on display, under dim light, in the Trésor (treasury) of the cathedral. This pair is hand-knitted in fine silk and are said to date from the fifteenth century. The patterns in the fabric are knitted with a contrasting fine metallic thread which has a silk core. The gauntlet has a deep border in scrolling patterns, reminiscent of brocade, while the backs of the hands have a large

Museum, close by the cathedral. This pair is plainly knitted in white silk, and the backs of the hands have metallic, enamelled circles representing religious subjects, in this case St Paul on the right hand and the Virgin Mary on the left. The cuffs are decorated with embroidery in coloured silks and gold thread. According to Elizabeth Coatsworth and Gale Owen-Crocker, who have studied these gloves closely in their 2018 book, *Clothing the Past: Surviving Garments from Early Medieval to Early Modern Western Europe*, these gloves are a composite of work; from the twelfth to the thirteenth centuries for the enamel plaques; the embroidery is 'thought to be fourteenth or fifteenth century', while the knitted gloves themselves probably fall somewhere between these dates.

Later examples of liturgical gloves demonstrate that knitting in two colours could be used to create elaborate patterns and religious symbols. Making these would have been much easier to do with 'real' knitting than with the looping techniques, employing the stranded method of two-colour knitting still used today.

Liturgical gloves have survived because of their costly materials and high status, sometimes being linked to a named bishop, and found in tombs and burials, often in fragments. They can have spiritual value, and have also been kept in cathedral treasuries where they are occasionally on display, such as those in Toulouse, already discussed, and a red and gold pair in the *Trésor* of the cathedral of St Bertrand de Comminges, illustrated. Some are associated with a particular saint, although usually the dates of the saint and those of the glove do not match, as was seen in the case of 'Saint Remi's' gloves in Toulouse.

A view of the cathedral of St Bertrand de Comminges.

The liturgical gloves of Bishop Pierre de Foix in the Trésor of St Bertrand de Comminges Cathedral. (With permission of Marcel Baurier, priest and rector of the Cathédral Sainte-Marie of St-Bertrand de Comminges)

eight-pointed snowflake or sunburst roundel enclosing the Christogram *IHS,* a symbol of Christ. The fingers and thumb all have two or three rings of complicated patterned gold knitted in. They are truly sumptuous! They are knitted at a gauge of 90 stitches per 10cm (23 stitches per inch), and 110 rounds per 10cm (28 rounds per inch). They are in very good condition and are said to have belonged to Cardinal Pierre de Foix, a French Roman Catholic bishop and cardinal from the fifteenth century.

Liturgical gloves are found in museums and collections in the UK, continental Europe and the USA, as well as in the treasuries of cathedrals. A significant group of liturgical gloves is held by the Glove Collection Trust, an organization linked to the Worshipful Company of Glovers of London. Their collection can be seen on-line, of which more in Chapter 5.

There are about one hundred pairs of knitted liturgical gloves still in existence, and irrespective of their religious significance, they are incredible examples of the knitters'

skill, not to mention the expertise of the producers of the fine silk threads, the metallic threads, the dyers of the threads, and the makers of the fine smooth needles that must have been necessary for this work. Further skill is shown in the additional ornamentation that many of them display: enamel medallions, beads, embroidery, fabric gauntlets, tassels, lace, braids and fringes are all found. However, not all these embellishments are usually present on one pair!

The makers of these gloves are unknown. None of the tools that the knitters used has survived the centuries. Making thread so fine with such a depth of colour would be difficult even now, with the benefit of modern techniques. Most information about them suggests that they were made in Spain or Italy, but no further detail is ever given.

See the information in the box about the Holy Hands research project for more about liturgical gloves, and how to see more examples of them.

The Holy Hands Research Project

This research project, carried out between March 2020 and November 2021, was funded by a grant from the Society of Antiquaries of London. It was conducted by a small team: Dr Angharad Thomas, Lesley O'Connell Edwards, independent researcher, and Sylvie Odstrčilová from the Czech Republic. The project was mentored by Dr Jane Malcolm-Davies, Knitting in Early Modern Europe (KEME), and the database was constructed by Jodie Cox of Wildside media. The result is a database of extant knitted liturgical gloves, with nearly one hundred entries. These are available to browse on the KEME website (see the Resources section at the back of the book for link). Note that the user is required to sign in, but the site is free to use. Most of the gloves are pairs, but there are some single ones, and a few that survive only as fragments. Details of them are recorded on the database, and there are links to on-line catalogues and websites where many of the gloves can be viewed.

Other materials that resulted from the Holy Hands project are available through the KEME website. The review of all the writings about liturgical gloves includes material in French, German and Dutch. There are also downloadable sheets on which to record information about gloves, including their measurements to be used when studying them.

The Holy Hands research project is the first to bring information about knitted liturgical gloves into one place, and it is hoped that it will form the foundation for more work about them.

Do visit it! (https://kemeresearch.com)

Guilds and Glove Making

Guilds were formed from the twelfth and thirteenth centuries onwards, in the UK and in other European countries, to promote and protect their particular trades. The Worshipful Company of Glovers of London was founded in 1349, but its main focus was on the making of leather gloves. However, the wording on its coat of arms is appropriate for any glove maker: it is 'True Hearts and Warm Hands'! Hand knitting did not fall into the remit of any of the medieval guilds; however, frame knitting, which is done on a machine, has a guild that is active to the present (see Resources).

Other Gloves

Before moving on to look at some of the gloves that have survived the years, it is worth pointing out that it is likely that many other types of item were knitted as the technique became more widely known. Just as it is today, knitting had the advantages of being stretchy and easier to do than the knotting or looping methods of making fabric, and was therefore ideal for gloves and mittens, socks and stockings and headgear. Most of these would have been made for ordinary working people, and as such would have been worn, and mended, to destruction.

The only surviving examples of early knitting that do not belong to extremely important people such as royalty, high clergy or the aristocracy are often just fragments. These turn up in odd places, including rubbish heaps, middens, and in one case, in a former latrine! Ironically, the anaerobic (without oxygen) conditions in these unlikely places are often suitable for the preservation of textile fibres made of protein, which includes wool. So those pieces that are still with us are just the tip of the knitting iceberg, as it were. These scraps that are left give tantalizing fragments of the story of knitting through the centuries, but with long gaps between them.

The 'Sture' Glove

The knitted artefacts that have come down through the centuries tend to be quite well known because there are so few. The famous 'Sture' glove dates from 1565, and its story has been told by various knitting authors, changing as more information is found about it and the interpretation of that information changes. This single silk glove is part of the collection of Sture family clothes kept in Uppsala Cathedral, Sweden, where it is usually on view. The glove is kept with clothing that belonged to other members of the Sture family, prominent Swedish nobility, who were murdered in 1567.

Quite a lot is known about the Sture glove because it was attached to the hat of the person it was given to, seemingly as a love token. That person was Sten Svantesson Sture, who died in a sea battle off the German coast in 1565 when the

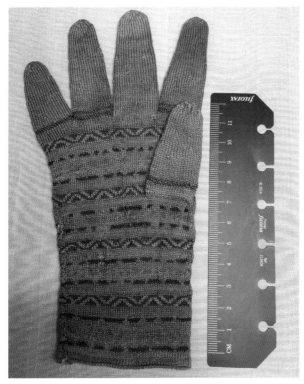

Knitted silk glove (palm), 1550–1570, The Cathedral Museum, Uppsala, Sweden, inventory number D10416. (© Jane Malcolm-Davies. Permission from Anna Ehn Lundgren, conservator, The Cathedral Museum, Uppsala, Sweden and Dr Jane Malcolm-Davies, UK)

Knitted silk glove (back of the hand), 1550–1570, The Cathedral Museum, Uppsala, Sweden, inventory number D10416. (© Jane Malcolm-Davies. Permission from Anna Ehn Lundgren, conservator, The Cathedral Museum, Uppsala, Sweden and Dr Jane Malcolm-Davies, UK)

ship of which he was the captain sank. However, his hat, and the (g)love token were saved for posterity.

The Sture glove is for a small right hand, being only 7cm (2.75in) across the palm. It is knitted in fine coloured silks and gold thread in stocking stitch, in the round. Patterned from the lower edge up, in bands of colourwork, it has the letters FREVCHEN SOFIA knitted around the hand, although these are hard to identify from photographs, being worked in a negative space pattern, the letters showing in the ground fabric. The fingers and thumb are tapered, and except for the middle finger, have rings of gold knitted into them. It has a gauge of 100 stitches and 100 rounds per 10cm/25 stitches and rounds per inch. The thumb construction is a peasant one, being set horizontally into the palm of the hand (*see* Chapter 1, 'Thumb Constructions').

The colours of the glove now appear to be a neutral (grey or beige) background, possibly faded from red, with patterns in yellow, green and orange. It is still a very lovely piece of knitting, using fine silk and gold thread to execute complicated patterns, finely and neatly knitted, perhaps knitted by the presumed donor or perhaps the product of a workshop or professional knitter?

The knitted-in words FREVCHEN SOFIA translate from the Swedish of the time as 'Princess Sofia'. Some sources interpret the V as a U and translate FREVCHEN as meaning 'miss' in middle German. However, this seems not to be the case here, as a suitable princess Sofia can be identified. Born in 1547, it was she, perhaps, who was the knitter of the Sture glove. She then gave it as a love token or favour for Sten Svantesson Sture, her possible future husband, who took it into battle with him, where it survived having been attached to his hat.

Silk Gloves – the Same but Different

Two pairs of ornately patterned silk gloves are shown in the illustration that opens the chapter. They are also available to see on the Glove Collection Trust (GCT) on-line catalogue using their numbers to search for them. These are two pairs of exceptionally beautiful knitted gloves in multicoloured silk. Both have a cream ground, and on it, scrolling, ornate patterns of leaves, flowers, animals and birds in shades of green, blue and pink and other colours.

At a glance, side by side in their boxes, they are strikingly similar. However, the pair shown in its box (GCT 23415) in the illustration is labelled as 'menswear' and date from 1700–1725, while the pair at the front (GCT 23413) is identified as 'ecclesiastical' and date from between 1675 and 1699. If these dates are correct, and many dates of clothing and costume are often estimates, then the two pairs are almost the same age. They certainly look very similar, the colours being almost identical, and the fineness and skill of the knitting being the same.

The main difference between them is that the pair GCT 23413 has the IHS initials, a symbol of Christ, as is so often found on the back of the hands of liturgical gloves, as we saw earlier in this chapter. This pair has further embellishment, being edged with bobbin lace made with metallic thread around the cuff and up the side of the gauntlet. It is fascinating to see the worlds of fashion and religion being connected in this way!

A similar pair of gloves to these is found in the collection of the Textile Museum and Documentation Centre (Centre de Documentació i Museu Tèxtil, CDMT) in Terrassa, a former centre of the textile industry, north-west of Barcelona, Catalonia. One of four pairs of liturgical gloves in this large collection of costume and textiles, these gloves are also richly patterned with scrolling plants, flowers and leaves, with a shield shape on the back of both hands. The most extraordinary feature of them is the letters that are knitted into the fingers to make words.

These gloves have been studied closely by Silvia Carbonell, and an illustrated leaflet about them is available on-line entitled 'Episcopal gloves with a message' (see Bibliography). In this publication it is argued that these might have belonged to a monk called Fray Agustin Lopez, who may even have knitted them himself. However, there turned out to be two people of this name, but it is thought more likely that the later one was the owner of these extraordinary gloves. They are,

like the others with these rich decorations, knitted extremely finely from very fine silk. There are several high-quality images of these gloves in the booklet, which dates them from the last quarter of the seventeenth century – that is, 1675–1699, and contemporary with the liturgical gloves GCT 23413 discussed above.

These three pairs of gloves, dated from 1675–1725, are from almost exactly the same decades as the pair that follows. But from the sun of southern Europe, we now go to the northernmost reaches of the British Isles, to the mainland of Shetland.

The 'Gunnister Man' Gloves

More than a century after the Sture glove, and also associated with the demise of the owner, the gloves that belonged to Gunnister man survive to add to knitting history. The misfortune of an unknown traveller in a remote part of the world led to the clothes that he was wearing being preserved. These clothes and a few other artefacts have been

The fingers of the Fray Agustìn gloves spelling out words. Image 20125(1) (© Museu Tèxtil de Terrassa/Quico Ortega)

Map of Shetland showing the location of Gunnister man's burial.

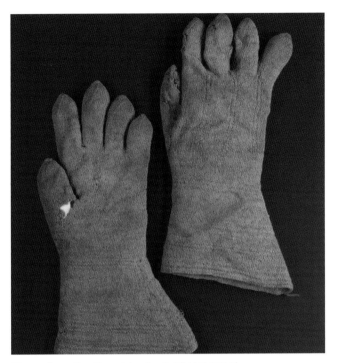

Gloves from the Gunnister burial (H.NA 1044).
(National Museums Scotland)

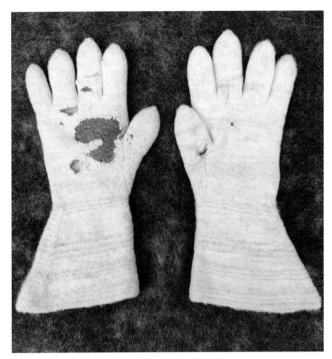

A reconstruction of Gunnister man's gloves, palms up.
(Shetland Museum and Archives)

a source of great interest for textile and fashion historians as they are datable with a good degree of accuracy. Their other point of interest is that they belonged to an ordinary person, rather than to someone in the upper echelons of society, from whom the vast majority of existing costume and textiles are preserved. The wearer of these textiles is known as 'Gunnister man', after the part of Shetland where he was found (*see* map).

His body had mostly vanished in the extremely acid peat bog into which he must have fallen, or perhaps been buried, in the seventeenth century. Due to the vagaries of bog preservation, only fragments of bone, some hair, and some finger and toenails were left when he was found by peat diggers in 1951. However, the clothes he had been wearing at the time of his burial had survived well. They were a coat and breeches of woven wool cloth, with knitted items in wool, including gloves, one of which was still on his hand, the other by his side. There were a few other personal possessions, including some coins. These enabled the dating of his demise to the late seventeenth century, 1680–90, an unusually precise date.

The knitted pieces surviving were two caps, stockings, a purse, and a pair of gloves. The purse is notable as it had colour work patterns knitted into its fabric, but it is the gloves

that are of interest here, knitted in one colour of wool. The gloves, not in a good condition even before their immersion in the peat bog, had been patched with cloth, are patterned with textured stitches, and have a pronounced gauntlet, the fashion of the period.

The original gloves are in the National Museum of Scotland, Edinburgh, where they were taken with all the artefacts from the burial following their discovery, and are shown in the image. However, in a joint project between Shetland Museum and the National Museum of Scotland, a replica set of Gunnister man's clothes was made in 2009, including the gloves.

Gunnister man's gloves were described in some detail in the *Proceedings of the Antiquaries of Scotland* in 1954, and are said to be knitted in soft brown wool. However, research during the reconstruction project showed that they had been originally knitted in white wool, the colour having changed due to immersion in the peat. They were knitted in the round on four needles, and the fingers were constructed 'as is usually practised today' according to the report, which dates from the time of the discovery. The gloves have purl ridges around the gauntlets and purl stitches in vertical lines on the back of the hands.

In knitting terms, these gloves were the product of an accomplished knitter who had the skills to produce a shaped gauntlet, a thumb gusset, and textured detail features. There is a pattern available for these gloves on-line. Finally, a notable but rather gruesome fact about these gloves is that some of Gunnister man's fingernails were found in the fingers!

The reconstruction shown here is a contemporary one, knitted and then distressed to simulate the wear by Dr Carol Christensen of the Shetland Museum and Archives.

A Hiatus in the Glove Record

According to knitting historian Irene Turnau, five-finger gloves became more common across Europe from the sixteenth century, as she says in her book from 1991, *History of Knitting before Mass Production*. Apart from those of the élites, such as the liturgical gloves, the gloves that have been preserved seem to be knitted in a single colour, rather than patterned, although this assertion is based on the very few examples that are still extant. One of these is a pair knitted in white cotton, with a flared cuff or gauntlet, in the collection of Herefordshire Museums. The pair is dated 1660–1685, more or less contemporary with Gunnister man's gloves. There are others in Scandinavian museums.

However, from the late eighteenth century onwards, a few pairs of gloves have survived that are knitted using more than one colour of yarn. Is it perhaps that feature – being knitted in more than one colour – that led to them being preserved? Might that have been unusual? There are references to gloves knitted in more than one colour in some writings on rural life in the UK from approximately this period, although again, these are frustratingly glancing.

The next pair to be observed is an example of a patterned glove, now across the North Sea in the northern Netherlands.

Dutch Gloves from 1783 with Mystery Cuff

This pair of gloves is the first of several dating from the late eighteenth century that have a name or initials and a date knitted in. This might be taken as an indication of how special these gloves were, that they should be marked with the owner's name and a date, presumably to ensure their return in case of being lost or mislaid. The tradition still continues at the present time, as we will see in later chapters.

Knitted gloves and mittens from the collection of the Fries Museum, Leeuwarden (T11154 & T07262K). (Fries Museum, Leeuwarden/Loan Ottema-Kingma Stichting)

A pair of wool gloves in the collection of the Fries Museum, Leeuwarden, the capital of the northern province of Friesland, northern Netherlands, is a real mystery. Despite the pair having a date, 1783, and initials, A.I., knitted into the back of each glove, separated by a rather splendid star, there is no further information. Assuming that the date is correct, their age is more or less all that is known about them. The maker of these gloves must have wanted to identify them beyond doubt, as the owner's, or perhaps the knitter's, initials are also knitted in. Both date and initials are on the back of each hand and would appear upside down to the wearer. The palms are knitted in the brown and cream 'speckle' pattern that surrounds the motifs on the back of the hand. This pattern differs on the back and the front of the hands, the stitches being alternated every round on the front of the hand, but every two rounds on the backs.

These gloves would fit a large hand, being 26cm (10.25in) long and 11cm (4.25in) across the palm. Knitted in brown and cream undyed, fine, evenly spun wool, it would be easy to think that this yarn was mechanically spun, but given the date of the gloves, 1783, this is not possible. Therefore the wool must have been hand spun to a high quality. The knitted fabric, in a small geometric pattern that surrounds the motifs, is also evenly worked. The construction of the fingers is not overly sophisticated – the fingers have some extra stitches to give width, but no actual gussets. The thumb is shaped, however, and decorated with a smaller star, fitted into the gusset.

Another very striking feature of the pair is the decorative cuff, made with multiple strands of the same wool used in the knitting, looped into swags. Other gloves from around this period sometimes have a fringe at the cuff edge, and sometimes further up the cuff too, but no others, apart from a tiny pair knitted for a baby or doll perhaps, in the same museum, have been found with this decoration. They can both be seen in the photograph, taken in the study room of the museum. No other examples of this trim have been found, despite extensive enquiries from the curatorial team at the museum.

The gloves have some damage, perhaps from moths in the past, but the wear has been mended with darning and some catching together of the fabric.

Gloves that Look Like Samplers

A Pair from 1835

Embroidered samplers are one of the best known types of textile, with their attractive assortment of alphabets, names and dates, often intermixed with flowers and animals. It is therefore not surprising to find similar motifs and patterns appearing on knitted gloves. A pair of gloves in the Hopkins Collection, London, has all-over patterns in small geometric designs, with a date, 1835, and a name, Marianne Clarke, knitted in around the wrists. This charming pair of gloves is knitted in wool: red on a background of black. The cuff edge is finished with a fringe.

The gloves are very neatly knitted with the thumbs having additional patterning on the gussets, the patterning carrying all the way up the fingers. They are small, as so many pairs of historic gloves are, being 18cm (7in) in length, and 9cm (3.5in) across the hand. They are knitted to a gauge of 50 stitches per 10cm (12 stitches per inch) approximately. The pair is in good condition, apart from a gap in the fringe of one glove. However, sadly, like the pair from the Fries Museum, nothing is known of its provenance. The pair came into the collection having been bought at auction by the collector.

Gloves Knitted for a Lord

A pair with similar sampler-type patterns of birds and flowers is to be found in the collection of Leicester Museums and Galleries. Leicester is a city in the English Midlands with a long connection to the textile trade, in particular the production of knitwear, which was made in factories close to the city centre as recently as the 1980s. This pair of gloves is a fine example of hand knitting, although yet again, little or nothing is known about the maker. The gloves also include a name and date, knitted in around the cuff: 'LORD HOWICK M.P.' and '1833'. Museum records show that they came into the collection in 1891 and were donated by a 'Mr Wm. Brown'.

Marianne Clarke's gloves, The Hopkins Collection, London. (The Hopkins Collection: Alan Hopkins)

The knitted gloves of Lord Howick. (Leicester City Council)

The gloves themselves are very attractive, with 'sampler'-type motifs knitted in three colours: crowns, plants in pots, hearts and birds all appear in rows around the hands, while the fingers are decorated with small geometric patterns in red and a dark colour, all on a background of white. Knitted in worsted wool in white and three contrast colours, red, blue and green, the construction is simple, with a peasant thumb and no finger gussets. Having examined them in person, Richard Rutt, the author of *A History of Hand Knitting*, noted that the 'tension is 6 stitches to the centimetre in the plain stocking stitch and 7 over the colour patterns'. They were possibly never worn, being relatively small for a man's hand.

A further piece of information linked to these gloves is that another title held by Lord Howick was Earl Grey, of the eponymous tea. It will probably never be known who knitted them, why they knitted them, or why they appear to be unworn. However, the inclusion of a date and initials, found on this pair and the previous two examples, give the knitting historian some clues with which to start researching.

The Gloves of G. Walton

The date on Lord Howick's gloves, 1833, is only thirteen years before that on the gloves in the collection of the Wordsworth Trust in Grasmere, Cumbria, which have the date '1846' knitted in around the wrist, along with the name 'G. Walton'. These are like the Dutch example already discussed, and also some of those made north of the border in Sanquhar,

The backs of the gloves belonging to G. Walton in the Wordsworth, Grasmere. (By permission of The Wordsworth Trust, Grasmere)

Scotland, being knitted in undyed dark and light pure wool, with a small geometric pattern. Their cuffs, however, have a fringe, a feature of some high-fashion gloves from earlier centuries, as well as gracing the pair that belonged to Marianne Clarke, and some other gloves in Estonia.

A reconstruction of the G. Walton gloves, along with some research about who he might have been, undertaken by textile historian Penelope Hemingway, is to be found as an addendum to the 2014 edition of the *Old Hand Knitters of the Dales* (*see* Bibliography).

Knitting in the North of England and Yorkshire

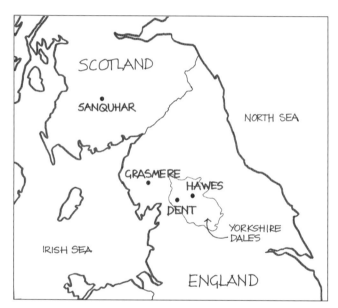

Location of knitting places and museums in England and Scotland.

The Rural Knitting Industry in the Dales

The 1846 gloves belonging to G. Walton were, if knitted locally, part of the production of the hand-knitting industry once widespread across the Yorkshire Dales.

In common with other rural upland communities in the UK, sheep were, and still are, ever present in the landscape. As in rural Wales and other upland areas of England and Scotland, in the eighteenth and nineteenth centuries people made a living as best they could using what was to hand. In the Yorkshire Dales, sheep were reared on the extensive hills so there was plenty of local wool available for hand knitting. Most of the inhabitants were farmers of one scale or another. There was also a mining industry, scattered across the Dales wherever deposits were worth exploiting. In the Dales, this was almost always lead.

So the isolated population had three sources of potential income: farming, lead mining and hand knitting. These they balanced according to the various prices and costs of yarn or stockings, farm produce and lead, which all varied according to the weather and market demand, itself often dependent on whether there was a war being fought, meaning demand for stockings for soldiers would be strong. Farmland would be taken in or out of use, and activities would vary due to these external forces – and because knitting was portable and could be done by most people including men, women and children, it could be managed to fit as necessary with the demands of other work.

The Lakes poet, Robert Southey, talked about 'The Terrible Knitters of Dent' because there was such a lot of knitting done there – 'terrible' being used in the sense of there being a great deal, rather than the quality not being good. Dent will be returned to as the home of the last known Dales knitter, Mary Allen.

Although wool was plentiful, its supply was controlled by the agents who organized the work of the knitters, bringing the yarn to them and taking away the finished goods. Little or nothing survives of this activity, all the products being the kind of garment that would wear out and be reprocessed into rags or otherwise recycled (not that it would have been called that, two centuries ago). The produce of this industry would have been destined for areas outside the Dales in any case, only garments for personal use being retained. Patterned gloves were also produced, but based on the evidence of the number of pairs that survive, it is likely that they were only ever made in very small numbers.

Knitting Methods in Rural Yorkshire

Records show that most of the knitting in the Yorkshire Dales produced coarse stockings knitted for soldiers. The 1846 gloves are a rare exception. The stocking knitting, being produced for strictly economic necessity and therefore to be executed as fast as possible, was done with the aid of a knitting stick or sheath. Needles were said to be fashioned from available wire by the local blacksmith and were double pointed, often with a curve. It is known that gloves were knitted using this method in the twentieth century, and presumably they were knitted like this before then, although on finer wires or needles. Examples of both the knitting sheaths and the needles are pictured here in the Dales Countryside Museum in the small Wensleydale town of Hawes.

Knitting sheaths and sticks in the Dales Countryside Museum, Hawes, North Yorkshire. (Photo courtesy of Dales Countryside Museum. Copyright Yorkshire Dales National Park Authority)

Curved knitting needles in the Dales Countryside Museum, Hawes, North Yorkshire. (Photo courtesy of Dales Countryside Museum. Copyright Yorkshire Dales National Park Authority)

Other Nineteenth-Century Gloves in Yorkshire

Thanks to the work of Marie Hartley and Joan Ingilby in their book *The Old Hand Knitters of the Dales* we know about other patterned gloves besides the G. Walton pair. Hartley and Ingilby travelled around the Yorkshire Dales observing its life and documenting through writing and illustration what they saw. They noted two other pairs of gloves from the nineteenth

century. The first of these they saw in Wensleydale, which they describe like this: 'The name on the wristband is Mary Moore's and the date is 1841.' Hartley and Ingilby continue: 'Mauve and scarlet wools have been used, with green and white stitches in the centres of the pattern on the back and a green fringe.' Regrettably this pair is not illustrated in their book and doesn't seem to have survived.

A further pair, seen by Hartley and Ingilby in Swaledale, has the name S. Hunter knitted in, and is dated to around 1850; it was knitted in black and red wool, and each glove also had a fringe, as shown in the drawing. In an article in *The Knitter* magazine, Penelope Hemingway established from census records that this pair was knitted by Sarah Hunter at the age of about twelve, and kept by her daughter, Miss H. Banks. The pair was illustrated in *The Old Hand Knitters of the Dales* but seems to have been lost in the intervening years. This pair is also the subject of a blog post by Ann Kingstone (*see* Resources). We will hear more of Hartley and Ingilby in the next chapter.

The gloves of S. Hunter.

Textile Production in Southern Scotland

The earliest patterned gloves in Scotland, in the Sanquhar area, also seem to date from the middle of the nineteenth century, and, like those in the Yorkshire Dales, emerged from a background of textile production. Sanquhar is situated in a rural upland area of southern Scotland and was therefore ideal for the production of wool textiles, having sheep and water-power. The textile industry in the form of weaving is recorded in Nithsdale, the valley in which Sanquhar is located, and Sanquhar itself from the Middle Ages. Not all economic activity in Nithsdale was of a rural variety however, as there was a small coal mine nearby and a carpet factory very near Sanquhar. Lead was also mined in the hills outside the town, an activity also pursued in the Yorkshire Dales in the seventeenth and eighteenth centuries.

The weaving trade is also recorded as the occupation of some of the deceased, on their gravestones in the local graveyard; furthermore knitting sold as 'Sanquhar stockings' and 'Sanquhar gloves' is mentioned as a curiosity of the town in a gazetteer of the nineteenth century, with hints that these could have been patterned. Were these the foundations of the gloves for which Sanquhar has become internationally famous?

Sanquhar is surrounded by the Scottish countryside.

Sanquhar Gloves

However, knitting as a domestic activity most often done by women in the home has often been overlooked in official records all over the world. The knitting of patterned gloves in Sanquhar or the vicinity is not specifically recorded until the mid-nineteenth century. A pair of gloves, recognizably Sanquhar Duke pattern, was part of a collection, that of a local historian, Dr Grierson, who died in 1889. This is perhaps the oldest pair of Sanquhar gloves extant, although this attribution has to be made with extreme caution as the evidence base is scanty.

Over the years, the knowledge and skills to knit Sanquhar gloves have been furthered by several people and events which, taken together, have ensured their continued production.

One such person was the Duke of Buccleuch, one of the largest landowners in Scotland and the owner of many acres around Sanquhar. Hearing that the glove knitters were experiencing difficulties, he placed a large order for gloves around 1880 in order to revive and sustain the industry.

By the mid-nineteenth century visitors were coming to Sanquhar and its environs, able to travel there by train, and attracted by the rural pursuits of shooting and fishing. Warm wool gloves would be ideal for these activities – even in the summer, gloves can be necessary in southern Scotland. Add to this the possibility of having a pair knitted with particular initials and a date, and they became an ideal souvenir and gift to take back home.

Gloves from Dr Grierson's collection in Dumfries Museum. (Image courtesy of Dumfries Museum)

Patterned knitted gloves from Sanquhar have survived from the nineteenth century, perhaps kept and valued because of their scarceness? With their dates and initials, and obviously skilled knitting, a pair of these gloves would have been a treasured possession, objects for safe keeping. We will return to the knitting of Sanquhar gloves in the twentieth century in Chapter 3.

Knitting in Estonia

The same trends were apparent in other areas of Europe where hand knitting was done, such as the Baltic states. From archaeological evidence found in what is now Estonia, knitting is known to have existed in northern Europe from the thirteenth to fourteenth centuries, the oldest fragment still in existence being probably the cuff of a mitten or glove in wool. By the eighteenth century, in Estonia people were knitting mittens in 'white and sheep brown' according to a historian of Estonian knitting.

The Estonian National Collection has over three thousand pairs of gloves and mittens, mainly dating from the nineteenth and twentieth centuries, although a few are recorded as being earlier. A single wool glove dated 1791, shown (ERM 2152/ab), has a white knitted lace hand and fingers, and a narrow cuff in wavy stripes of dark blue and white. The white is the natural white of the sheep's wool, and the dark blue is most likely derived from indigo dye.

Another pair in lace knitting from the same collection (ERM 7708) has a patterned and textured cuff in three colours; this pair is dated 1837. The fine lace patterns that can be seen on the side of the hand of each glove, shown palm upwards, continue on the back of it.

Dated 1851, another pair of gloves (ERM 1439/ab) demonstrates a complex cuff in four colours with both a fringe and knitted braid, while the hands, thumbs and fingers are patterned all over in both large and small geometric motifs. Even in the nineteenth century, knitted Estonian gloves were demonstrating many complex techniques, including colour-stranded knitting, entrelac, chevron stripes in lace, and inlay or *roositud* – all of these sometimes complemented with fringes and contrasting fingertips. Gloves were necessary for warmth in the northern winter, but were also a key component of the national costume, which was gaining importance through the nineteenth century as the founding of the modern state was taking place. The wonderful gloves of Estonia will be returned to in the next chapter; they can also be found on-line.

Conclusion

Gloves have played an important role in marking the story of the history and development of knitting. Some of the earliest textiles known to be made in true knitting are the

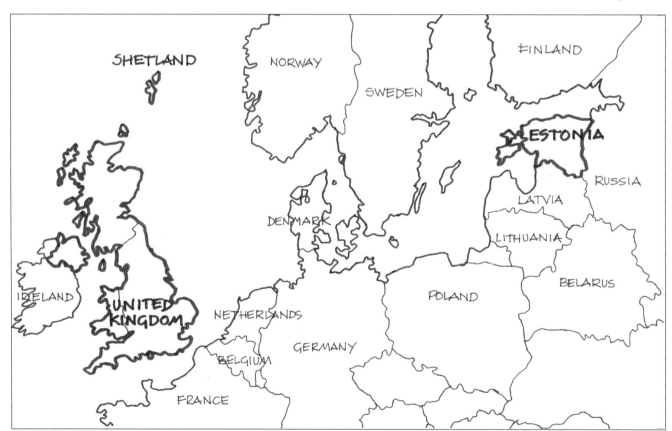

Map showing northern Europe and Estonia.

The back of a right glove dated 1791 from the collection of the Estonian National Museum, Tartu (ERM 2152/ab). (Creative Commons licence)

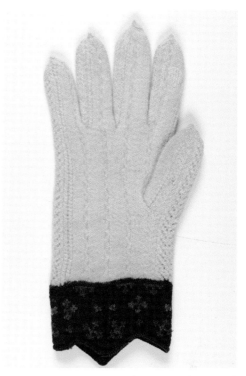

The right glove of a pair dated 1837 from the collection of the Estonian National Museum ERM 7708/ab. (Creative Commons licence)

Pair of gloves dated 1851 from the collection of the Estonian National Museum ERM 1439/ab. (Creative Commons licence)

liturgical gloves that still survive, which also include the most breath-taking examples of the knitters' art and craft. The fact that gloves exist that were made in looping techniques and then in true knitting show that knitting is a relatively recent addition to the textile crafts.

It is not known, and may never be known, how the technique of knitting in two colours to make intricate and beautiful hand coverings came about. The examples that are known, with their dates sometimes more than a century apart from each other, and found in different locations, seem to be unconnected. Is it the case, as in a Russian saying, that those who sit in the same draught, catch the same cold? Given wool, sheep with dark and light fleece, a method of turning this into yarn, the yarn into a fabric, and the fabric into a structure …. add cold weather, then perhaps patterned gloves are one possible outcome of anywhere possessing these conditions and resources? And of all the knitted socks, mittens worn to destruction in the course of hard work, were patterned gloves the items that were kept for posterity because they were so special?

Pattern 2: Inspired by History

Pattern 2: 'Inspired by History'.

Cuff detail.

Historical examples are the design inspiration for this pair of gloves. The pattern on the cuff is purl stitch diamonds, found in a pair of liturgical gloves in the collection of the Design Museum in Barcelona, while the pointed fingertips are similar to those of a pair in the Glovers Trust Collection. This pair is knitted in silk, like the early gloves, which although more difficult to work, being less stretchy than

wool, gives a warm fabric that also looks luxurious. It is also ideal for those who find wool hard to wear. The yarn specified has a wide range of colours. This pattern could also be knitted in other fine yarns such as a fine cashmere or in heavier yarns to give a larger glove.

There is a chart for the textured pattern around the wrist of these gloves, indicating the purl stitch pattern.

Materials

Yarn
BC Garn, Jaipur Silk Fino, 100% silk, 50g skein, 300m/328 yds, colour Jeansblau, shade 62, 1 skein.
Finished gloves weigh 40g and take 240m/262yds approx.

Needles
2mm knitting needles or size to achieve gauge (*see* Chapter 1 for types of knitting needle).

Tools
Stitch markers or lengths of contrasting yarn tied into loops.
Stitch holders and/or lengths of smooth strong contrasting yarn for holding stitches.
Wool sewing needle and scissors for finishing.

Finished size:
To fit a small/medium adult hand.
Length: 21cm/8.25in.
All round above thumb: 18cm/7in.

Tension/gauge:
48 sts and 56 rounds = 10cm/4in over stocking stitch knitted in the round.

Abbreviations:
See abbreviations list at back of book.

Special techniques:
See 'Techniques for Knitting Plain Gloves' in Chapter 1, which covers 'casting on for finger and thumb constructions: various ways'.

Instructions

Work both gloves the same until thumb placement (*).

Cuff
CO 78 sts using long tail thumb method.
Note, first 6 rows are knitted flat.
Row 1 (RS): Purl.
Knit 5 rows garter stitch, that is, every row knit.
Join to work into a round.

Knit 2 rounds.
Work 18 rounds from cuff chart, working chart twice in each round.

Knit 2 rounds plain (every st knit)*.

Right Glove
Place the Thumb.
Round 1: K46, p1, mark stitch, k31.
Round 2: K46, p1, M1 purlwise, (pick up thread between sts from front to back, place on left needle, purl into back of this,

k31. These purl sts are the edge sts of the thumb gusset. You may want to mark them.
Round 3: K46, p1, M1L, p1, k31.
Round 4: K46, p1, k1, M1L, p1, k31.
Round 5: K46, p1, k2, M1L, p1, k31.

Continue in this manner, increasing 1 st every round until there are 24 sts between the purl edge sts.

Make the thumb opening:
K46, put 26 sts onto on a length of contrast yarn, that is the 24 sts between the markers plus 1 st either side, CO 4 sts, K31; 81 sts.
Dec round: K45, ssk, K2, K2tog, K to end of round, 79 sts.
Knit on these sts until hand measures 4cm/1.5in from thumb opening.

Fourth finger:
K10, put 60 sts onto on a length of contrast yarn, CO5, K9 sts; 24 sts. Working in the round, K until finger measures 5cm/2in, or 0.5cm/0.25in shorter than length required.

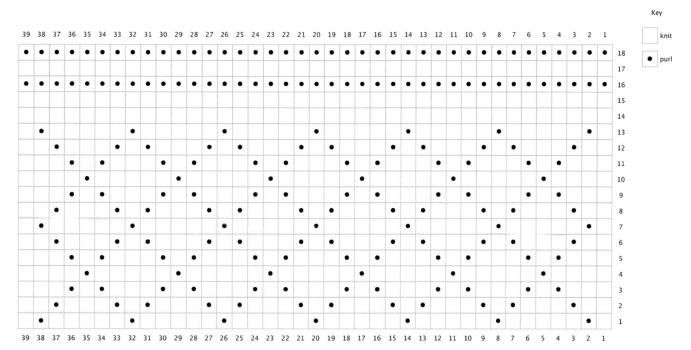

Pattern 2, cuff chart.

Shape tip
Round 1: (K6, k2tog) 3 times. 21 sts.
Round 2: (K5, k2tog) 3 times. 18 sts.
Continue decreasing in this way until 3 sts remain. Cut yarn, draw through sts, tighten and fasten off.

Extend hand:
Return to sts on a length of contrast yarn, re-join yarn, knit all round 60 sts, PUK 4 sts from base of fourth finger; 64 sts; K4 rounds.

Third finger:
K10, put 40 sts on to length of contrast yarn, CO2, K14 sts from contrast yarn; 26 sts. Working in the round, K until finger measures 5cm/2in or 0.5cm/0.25in shorter than length required.

Shape tip
Round 1: (K7, k2tog) 2 times, k8. 24 sts.
Round 2: (K6, k2tog) 3 times. 21 sts.
Round 3: (K5, k2tog) 3 times. 18 sts.
Continue decreasing in this way until 3 sts remain. Cut the yarn, draw through the sts, tighten and fasten off.

Second finger:
With palm facing, K10sts from contrast yarn, PUK 2 sts from base of third finger, K10 sts from contrast yarn, CO 4 sts; 26 sts. Working in the round K until finger measures 7cm/2.75in or 0.5cm/0.25in shorter than length required. Shape tip as third finger

First finger:
K20 sts from contrast yarn, PUK 6 sts from base of second finger; 26 sts. Working in the round, K until finger measures 6.5cm/2.5in or 0.5cm/0.25in shorter than length required. Shape tip as third finger.

Thumb:
K26 sts from contrast yarn, PUK 4 sts from thumb gusset; 30 sts. Working in the round, K until thumb measures 5cm/2in or 0.5cm/0.25in shorter than length required.

Shape tip
Round 1: (K8, k2tog) 3 times. 27 sts.
Round 2: (K7, k2tog) 3 times. 24 sts.
Continue decreasing in this way until 3 sts remain. Cut yarn, draw through sts, tighten and fasten off.

Left Glove
Work as right glove to*.

Place the Thumb
Round 1: K31, p1, mark stitch, k46.
Round 2: K31, M1L purlwise, p1, k46. These 2 sts are the edges of the thumb gusset. You may want to mark them.
Round 3: K31, p1, M1R, p1, k46.
Round 4: K31, p1, M1R, k1, p1, k46.
Round 5: K31, p1, k2, M1R, k2, p1, k46.
Continue in this manner, increasing 1 st every round until there are 24 sts between the purl edge sts.

Make the thumb opening:
K31, put 26 sts onto on a length of contrast yarn, that is the 24 sts between the markers plus 1 st either side, CO 4 sts, k46; 81 sts.
Dec round: K30, ssk, k2, k2tog, k to end of round; 79 sts.
Knit on these sts until hand measures 4cm/1.5in from thumb opening.

Fourth finger:
K9, slip 60 sts onto on a length of contrast yarn, CO 5 sts, K10 sts; 24 sts. Working in the round, K until finger measures 5cm/2in, or 0.5cm/0.25in shorter than length required.

Shape tip
Round 1: (K6, k2tog) 3 times; 21 sts.
Round 2: (K5, k2tog) 3 times; 18 sts.
Continue decreasing in this way until 3 sts remain. Cut yarn, draw through sts, tighten and fasten off.

Extend hand:
Return to sts on a length of contrast yarn, re-join yarn, knit all round 60 sts, PUK 4 sts from base of fourth finger; 64 sts; K4 rounds.

Third finger:
Work as for right hand third finger.

Second finger:
With back of hand facing, K10sts from contrast yarn, PUK 2 sts from base of third finger, K10 sts from contrast yarn, CO 4 sts; 26 sts. Working in the round K until finger measures 7cm/2.75in or 0.5cm/0.25in shorter than length required. Shape tip: As third finger.

First finger:

K 20 from contrast yarn, PUK 6 sts from base of second finger; 26 sts. Working in the round, K until finger measures 6.5cm/2.5in or 0.5cm/0.25in shorter than length required. Shape tip: As third finger.

Thumb:

Work as for right thumb.

Finishing:

Darn in all ends, closing any gaps at the base of the fingers as necessary. Use the tail from the cast on to stitch the ends of the first 6 rows together. Press the gloves with a cool iron and damp cloth or according to instructions with the yarn.

BT 01.22.

CHAPTER 3

PATTERNED GLOVES IN YORKSHIRE, SCOTLAND AND ESTONIA

Where are Colour-Patterned Gloves Found?

Having looked at the construction of a glove knitted in one colour in Chapter 1 and at some of the known historic examples of gloves, both plain and patterned, in Chapter 2, this chapter looks at gloves knitted in more than one colour after 1900 and up to the present day. Of course, patterns can be made with textured stitches as well as different colours of yarn, but in this chapter the focus is on gloves with colour patterns.

Knitting with more than one colour yarn forms a thicker fabric than one knitted in a single colour and is therefore ideal for articles where warmth is needed, such as hats, gloves and mittens. It almost goes without saying that these fabrics will be knitted in wool of some type, and although silk can also be warm, it doesn't tend to be as fluffy or comfortable to wear as wool. It's not surprising, therefore, that multicoloured knitted gloves are found, and still knitted, all over northern Europe and the cooler parts of North America.

In the UK, both southern Scotland and Yorkshire have traditions of knitting colour-patterned gloves, as do the Baltic countries, Estonia, Latvia and Lithuania. Scandinavia – taking that to include Sweden, Norway, Denmark and Finland, as well as Iceland, the Faroe Islands and Greenland – has rich colour-knitting traditions, which include gloves. The northern provinces of Newfoundland and Labrador, northern Canada, are also home to gloves knitted in colour patterns. A very finely knitted example is in the Ashmolean Museum, Oxford, said to have come from Kashmir, part of which is in the Himalayas and knitted from fine 'pashmina wool' in several colours.

Perhaps colour knitting is to be found wherever there is the sort of climate to need its warmth-preserving qualities, along with a supply of fibre from local flocks of sheep, cashmere goats or even yaks?

The gloves in the image are from Norway, left, and Shetland, right, from the collection of the Knitting & Crochet

Gloves from Norway (KCG Collection) and Shetland (Angharad Thomas Collection).

Guild and my personal collection respectively. The links between countries separated by sea or oceans often have a strong history, due to travel by ship, and it is clear from the similarities in these gloves that there has been interaction between the people of both places. The likenesses are noticeable in the patterns from the turned-back cuffs to the star on the back of the hands and the thumb construction. In addition, the patterns on the fingers are identical on the backs, while the palms have small all-over patterns that continue up the fingers. Both are knitted in the round in woollen spun pure wool in largely shades of undyed wool, although in the Norwegian pair there are some dyed colours, too.

We will see other similarities between patterned gloves from different places as we move from here to the Yorkshire Dales, Sanquhar in Scotland and then to Estonia.

This chapter starts by taking up the story of patterned gloves found in the UK, firstly in Yorkshire, then in southern Scotland, which were introduced in the last chapter, concluding at the end of the nineteenth century. Now the story moves into the twentieth century and on to the present day. The chapter ends by looking at patterned gloves found in Estonia, the most northerly of the Baltic countries.

For each area in this chapter – the Dales, Sanquhar and Estonia – aspects of glove history are explored, information about materials and construction given, and a pattern for knitting a glove inspired by each region is included.

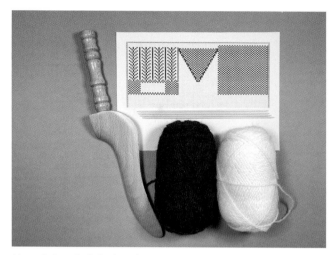

Materials to knit Dales gloves.

Sheep and lambs in the Yorkshire Dales.

Yorkshire Dales Gloves

How Do We Know about Dales Gloves?

Glove knitting in the Yorkshire Dales, and many other aspects of life in the region, were documented by Marie Hartley and Joan Ingilby in illustrated books published throughout the second part of the twentieth century. The nineteenth-century gloves recorded by them have been described in the previous chapter. In their books they observed daily life in rural Yorkshire, with photographs and drawings, the artefacts and tools used, and the goods produced. Marie Hartley was an artist who had trained at the Slade School of Art in London, and Joan Ingilby was a writer.

Both women were comfortably off to the extent that they could indulge their interest in their native county from a base in Wensleydale in the heart of the Yorkshire Dales National Park. One of the first books they wrote and illustrated together was *The Old Hand-Knitters of the Dales* published in 1951, subsequently revised, reprinted and republished through several editions, illustrated, the latest of which is dated 2014.

Their wide and deep explorations of the Yorkshire Dales, particularly in *The Old Hand-Knitters*, captured more or less all that is known about the Dales' rural knitting industry. This is an invaluable source for anyone interested in hand knitting, and includes an account of the history of knitting entitled 'Knitting in Early Times' in the first chapter. The book does not focus on the production of gloves in particular, since it examines all aspects of wool and knitting production in

The Old Hand-Knitters of the Dales *1951.*

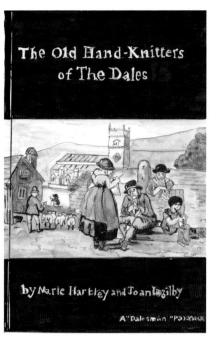

The Old Hand-Knitters of the Dales *1969.*

The Old Hand-Knitters of the Dales *1978.*

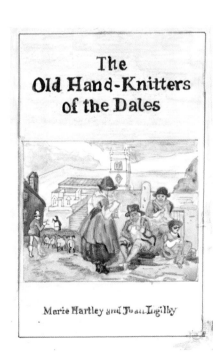

The Old Hand-Knitters of the Dales *1988.*

The Old Hand-Knitters of the Dales *2001.*

The Old Hand-Knitters of the Dales *2014.*

the Dales, much of it stockings which, as already stated, far outnumbered any other sort of goods produced. They also recorded that the amount of knitting activity in Dentdale in the eighteenth century caused Southey, the Lakeland poet, to call the townsfolk the 'terrible knitters of Dent', 'terrible' having a rather different connotation in that context, as in 'big' or 'important'.

Hartley and Ingilby nevertheless came across examples of gloves in their travels in the Yorkshire Dales, and also documented those already in the Wordsworth Museum in Grasmere. Two of these pairs they thought sufficiently noteworthy to record in rather attractive line drawings, along with two from the nineteenth century. One or two other pairs are mentioned, almost in passing, in discussing various dales. The information they give about glove knitting actually varies between the editions of *The Old Hand-knitters of the Dales,* it being more extensive in some editions than others.

What Were the Dales Gloves Like?

Of those gloves captured in line drawings by Marie Hartley, one of which is shown, all are knitted in two colours with geometric patterns, and initials or names and dates around the wrist. Three of the four are knitted in wool, and one in what is described as 'silk'. The dates knitted into the gloves range from 1846 to 1919. Two of the pairs are identified as being in the Wordsworth Museum, Grasmere, where they remain today.

Of this group, the oldest pair is that of G. Walton, previously described in Chapter 2. The two later pairs each have paper labels sewn to them, one indicating that it is the 'survivor of obsolete (sic) work of the Terrible Knitters of Dent' and the other 'made by Miss Allen of Dent'. Both pairs of gloves were donated by the owners or their relatives, who must have thought them notable enough to be lodged in what was possibly the only suitable place for them at the time, the focus of the Wordsworth Trust collection being papers related to the poet and his time at Dove Cottage.

Of the gloves that Hartley and Ingilby chose to illustrate in *The Old Hand-Knitters of the Dales,* two can be firmly identified as Dent or Mary Allen gloves, as they show the distinctive characteristics: the four columns of patterns on the back of the hand, the small geometric pattern used for the wrist, thumbs and fingers (the palms are not seen), the name and

M. Pearson's gloves, recorded by Hartley and Ingilby.

date around the wrist, and the fine vertical lines of the black and white ribbed cuff.

Dent and Mary Allen Gloves

Forty miles to the south-east of Grasmere, Dent is now a quiet village in the north Yorkshire Dales. Situated in the heart of its eponymous dale, it is the sort of place where a good hike might be started, or a pleasant rural day out be enjoyed. It has not always been like this, though. Dent in the eighteenth and nineteenth centuries was a busy centre of the hand-knitting trade, indeed the home of the 'terrible knitters'.

Dent was also the home of Miss Allen, the maker of the gloves now in Grasmere, earning her living as a 'glove knitter' according to the census return from 1911. Born in Dent in 1857, Mary Allen was probably one of the last people in the area to earn a living from knitting. She died in 1924, and

Cottages in the centre of Dent village.

Mary Allen, glove knitter of Dent, Yorkshire Archaeological and Historical Society, University of Leeds, Special Collections. (Marie Hartley Collection YAS/MS1803 Box 6)

The gloves are sometimes called 'Dales' gloves, sometimes 'Dent' gloves, and sometimes 'Mary Allen' gloves. Not all Dales gloves are in fact the work of Mary Allen, but apart from the 1846 G. Walton pair kept in Grasmere, all the other extant Dales-style gloves seem to have been knitted by her. These show the same features in their making, from the cast-on at the bottom edge of the cuffs to the tips of the fingers, which are shaped in the same way. Was Mary Allen the only knitter of Dent gloves?

Just a further note on naming and to clear up any confusions: there is a very well-known glove-making company in the UK that bears the name 'Dents'. There is no connection at all between the village and the manufacturing company, other than the production of gloves, of course.

Where Can Dales Gloves Still Be Found?

There are other Dales gloves still preserved for posterity, because in the course of their travels, Hartley and Ingilby collected artefacts, as well as recording their usage, in their investigations about Yorkshire Dales life. The Dales Countryside

The Dales Countryside Museum, Hawes, North Yorkshire.

the latest known gloves thought to have been knitted by her are dated 1919, therefore knitted when she was sixty-two years of age. Her mother was also recorded as a glove knitter in the censuses of 1861 and 1891.

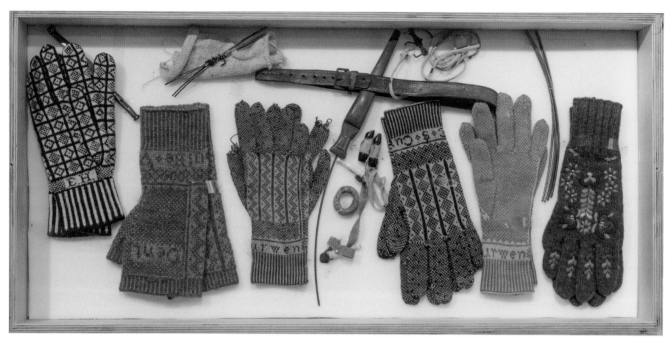

Hand-knitted gloves in the Dales Countryside Museum, Hawes, North Yorkshire. (Photo courtesy of Dales Countryside Museum. Copyright Yorkshire Dales National Park Authority)

The gloves knitted in 'art silk' by Mary Allen in the Dales Countryside Museum, Hawes. (Photo courtesy of Dales Countryside Museum. Copyright Yorkshire Dales National Park Authority)

Child's gloves with 'Joan' knitted in round the wrist. (Photo courtesy of Dales Countryside Museum. Copyright Yorkshire Dales National Park Authority)

Museum in the small town of Hawes in Wensleydale became the home of their collection, covering almost every aspect of life in the Dales. Fortunately for knitters everywhere this collection includes five pairs of gloves known to have been knitted by Mary Allen, along with other knitting-related artefacts such as knitting sheaths or sticks, and the distinctive curved needles, as shown in Chapter 2.

Curwen was the family name of the vicar in Dent, and a pair each was knitted for him, his wife and their two daughters, whose names were also knitted into their gloves. One pair of the Curwen gloves is knitted in a silky yarn, like one of the pairs in Grasmere. Labelled as 'silk' in *The Old Hand-Knitters of the Dales*, it is not known if this yarn is in fact silk or, as is more likely, an 'art' silk or rayon. This yarn would have become available at around the time these gloves were knitted, in the early decades of the twentieth century.

Another of the pairs in the Dales Countryside Museum was knitted in black and white wool, while the two pairs for the girls of the family were knitted in much lighter coloured wools – these seem to have faded with age to the extent that their patterns can hardly be seen. They, too, have their names knitted in around the wrists, Joan and Mary, although these are very faint, as can be seen in the photograph.

The 'Dent' or 'Mary Allen' gloves that survive in collections are knitted in one of two yarns: a fine, smooth wool or a silk or rayon, both of which appear to have been industrially spun and dyed. It will probably always be a mystery as to where the fine, smooth, factory-produced yarns came from, and how they reached Dent village.

All these gloves are very similar, the main variation being the patterns that go up the back of the hands. These are one of three – diamonds, tree of life, or a zigzag, *see* chart – and are worked over seven or nine stitches depending on the size of the glove.

These gloves, from the Yorkshire Dales, or Dent, are rare, perhaps fewer than twenty pairs being extant. It is believed by some who have studied this, that the few still existing in museums are the remains of many thousands of pairs of this style of glove that were knitted in the Yorkshire

Dales. In my opinion, these patterned gloves were only ever produced by a small number of people, including Mary Allen and her mother, identified in census data as glove knitters. Only some of these gloves have survived, and those that have are special enough to have been treasured by their owners and subsequently found their way into textile collections.

Keeping the Mary Allen Knitting Tradition Alive

The knitting researcher, collector and designer, Sue Leighton-White, studied the Mary Allen gloves in the collection of the Wordsworth Trust, Grasmere. She also interviewed Mary Allen's son, Canon Eric Allen, about his mother's glove knitting, which he remembered clearly from his boyhood. Sue then reconstructed the gloves and wrote a pattern for knitting them, which was sold through the shop at the Wordsworth Trust, but which is no longer available. An article giving this research was published in the American knitting magazine, *Piecework*, in 1994 and reprinted in *Knitting Traditions* in 2011. Both are available as digital downloads; however, only the 2011 magazine contains the instructions and charts for knitting the gloves (*see* Resources at the back of this book).

Why Knit a Replica?

Sue Leighton-White decided to knit a replica of one of Mary Allen's gloves from the Wordsworth Museum, Grasmere, as she explains in her article in *Knitting Traditions* winter 2011: 'To help preserve the fine work of a pair of gloves made by Dent handknitter Mary Allen.' Knitting a replica is surprisingly hard to do, as finding out how things have been made, once complete, is difficult. If the item being studied is an old or historic and therefore precious textile, then most likely it cannot even be touched when being analysed.

It is especially hard to determine how increasing and decreasing have been done, in fact, in these Dales gloves. The shapings that widen the hand are not obvious until the pattern is actually counted out, stitch by stitch. Once the position of any increases or decreases has been identified, the only way to find out how this operation was done is to attempt to copy it using needle and yarn. The pattern that Sue Leighton-White researched and documented is for a replica of gloves that Mary Allen knitted for a Mr H. Inglis, whose name is knitted in around the cuffs.

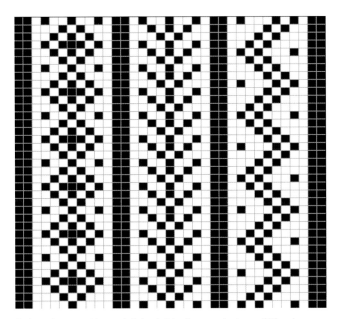

Dales gloves patterns, left to right: *diamonds, tree of life, zig-zag.*

Knitting a Pair of Dales Gloves

There are few patterns available. *Knitting Traditions* 2011, winter, published a feature and the pattern for Mary Allen gloves complete with charts. Both are available digitally: *see* Bibliography for details.

For the G. Walton gloves in the Wordsworth Trust a pattern with charts is included in *The Old Hand-knitters of the Dales*, 2014, reverse engineered by Penelope Hemingway.

Penelope Hemingway also designed a pattern for the gloves of Sarah Hunter in *The Knitter*, Issue 150: *see* Bibliography for details.

The Mary Allen Gloves in the Collection of the Knitting & Crochet Guild

Finally, we come to this pair of 'Dales' gloves from the collection of the Knitting & Crochet Guild. Knowing what we do about 'Dales' gloves, it can be seen that this pair is almost certainly the work of the same hands, those of Mary Allen – 'Miss Allen of Dent'.

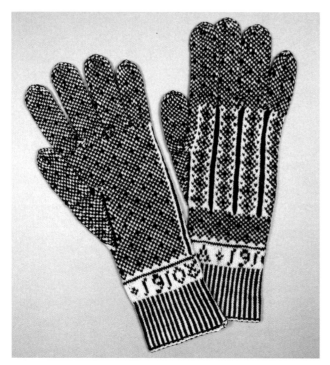

The 'Dent' gloves from the Knitting & Crochet Guild Collection.

This pair, in very good condition, shows all the 'Dales glove' features: knitted in two colours, black and white, in smoothly spun pure wool, giving an even, tight fabric to the glove. The lower edge of the cuff is formed of a cast-on in both the black and the white yarn, giving it a finely braided appearance. This pair (also typically) has a cuff in knit-one purl-one rib in black and white. Above this, around the wrist, initials and a year are knitted in: on this pair, M.E.A., 1910. The lettering on both cuffs is the same, but the initials show on the back of the hand of the right glove, whereas the date shows on the back of the hand of the left glove.

There are four columns of diamonds on the back of the hands, different from others in that they have a small, solid cross in the middle of the diamond, while the small all-over geometric pattern known as 'midge and flea' makes a band around the wrist and is used for the palms, the fingers and the thumbs.

The thumb is constructed with a shaped gusset that sits to the palm side of the hand, while the construction of the fingers is just a few stitches between the hand and the fingers themselves. The fingers and thumb are shaped at the top into blunt tips, while keeping the pattern of alternate-coloured stitches correct.

What is known about this pair of gloves, and why are they in a collection? The collection that contains this particular pair of Dales gloves is that of the Knitting & Crochet Guild (KCG), a UK-based membership organization that promotes the crafts of hand and machine knitting and crochet. Founded in 1978 by a group of enthusiasts for their crafts, since 1991 the KCG has actively collected examples of all aspects of these crafts: textiles of all kinds – garments, household textiles and art pieces; books, patterns and publications; tools and gadgets; and yarns and shade cards. The many thousands of items in the KCG Collection are held in a former textile mill near Huddersfield, Yorkshire.

The Story of the 'Dent Gloves'

According to the records in the KCG Collection, these gloves were bought for the collection in 2004 at an antique textile fair from a dealer who was based in Carlisle. The record says 'Hand knitted Dent gloves'. A handwritten note came with them, giving a little information about the owner of the gloves, Miss Isabel Clark, who was the headmistress of the primary school in Dent between 1945 and 1968.

The story of how they came into the collection has only recently been discovered more fully. When Miss Clark retired, she went to live next door to her sister in the Cumbrian village of Brampton. On Miss Clark's death in 1976, her sister had to clear the house. The gloves were found and given to another neighbour, who handed them on to her friend who was a textile dealer. They then came to the KCG from the dealer's stall at the Antique Textiles Fair held in Manchester, in September 2004.

The only remaining puzzle concerns the initials round the wrist of the gloves, M.E.A., which are obviously not those of Miss Isabel Clark. The date knitted into the wrist is 1910, most likely the year in which they were knitted, and presumably the original owner's initials were M.E.A. (It's tempting to think that these may have belonged to Mary Allen herself, but there is no evidence to confirm this.) Perhaps this was a person with a very small hand, as these gloves are only 9cm (3.5in) across the palm of the hands, making them very tight for all but the slimmest of hands.

Most of the story of the gloves' provenance can be told however, tracing their journey from Dent village, via Brampton and Carlisle in Cumbria, to Slaithwaite near Huddersfield, their current home.

This pair of gloves, being so narrow and in such good condition, may never have been worn. It was not unusual for very ornate gloves to be kept for 'best', when they might have been carried in the hand and not actually put on.

The pattern for the gloves that follows is not a replica of the one shown, but it is very much in the spirit of it. My replica alongside the original gloves is pictured, and the difficulties of creating a replica have already been discussed in the context of that of Sue Leighton-White's. The replica is too narrow for

most hands, even the slimmest. For the pattern that follows the size was made bigger to be more appropriate for modern hands. However, this pattern takes many features from that glove and incorporates them into one that will fit a larger hand, while displaying the distinctive characteristics of this piece of knitting history. The two-colour cast-on, the scope for initials and/or a date around the cuff, and the vertical patterns running up the back of the hand, are all found here.

This pattern uses solid coloured, plain yarns in black and an off-white, like the Mary Allen gloves. In composition it is 75 per cent wool with 25 per cent polyamide to give added wearing properties. The yarn specified is spun in Bradford, Yorkshire, and is hard wearing and good value. It also comes in a large range of colours. Of course other yarns could be used, but remember to check the weight of the yarn by looking at the length per unit weight when making a substitution.

Techniques for Knitting in Two Colours

All the construction techniques used in knitting the plain glove from Chapter 1 are used in this glove too. So if that glove, or any other, has been knitted, there should be a familiarity with 'glove basics' such as knitting in the round, shaping for the thumb, forming the thumb, and finally forming the fingers. Everything works in much the same way, but with two yarns rather than one! For example, when casting on for the thumb or the base of a finger, work the stiches in alternate colours and then both working yarns are in the right place to continue knitting.

Again, there are many videos on the internet that show all these techniques. Some are in slow motion so they are even easier to follow.

Two-colour Cast-ons

There are many techniques for casting on in two colours, giving various effects and degrees of stretch. Perhaps the simplest is to use the long tail thumb method, but starting with the two colours of yarn joined in a slip knot and then proceeding as usual. This gives stitches of one colour and a line of the other colour below.

Another suitable cast-on for a glove in two colours is the German twisted cast-on, of which there are many variations.

Original Dent glove, left, with replica, right.

Note: Do not struggle with a complicated two-colour cast-on at the expense of actually getting started knitting! Just use one colour, and then go on to two once the stitches are established on the needles.

Knitting in the Round with Two Colours

Knitting in two colours in the round is easier than knitting with two colours in flat knitting, as only knit stitches have to be worked. The yarns can be held in one of several ways: one colour in each hand, both colours in the left hand, or both in the right hand. Every knitter has to find their own way of doing this.

Increasing in the round: This is done in the usual way, but care may have to be taken to keep colour repeats correct. Charts will usually indicate which colour to work an increase.

Other Techniques

Other techniques include taking off on to threads/keeping stitches for later; casting on for finger and thumb constructions in various ways; joining back into the round; and pick-up and knit are techniques that were all discussed in Chapter 1. All of these processes are done in the same way as when using one colour – the secret is to keep alternating the yarns when doing them. For instance, when casting on for the base of a finger, work the first stitch in one colour and the second in the other one, then repeat. The same applies when picking up stitches at the base of the fingers.

Shaping fingertips and finishing: In colour work the decreasing needs to be worked to keep the colours correct, and instructions for doing this will be given in the pattern. For a simple speckle stitch or alternating colours, a knit three together followed by knit one does this.

Sewing in the ends and neatening the work: This is obviously twice as much work with two colours!

Pressing, blocking and washing: This is the same as for the plain gloves.

Knitting from a Chart

The pattern for the colourwork gloves that follows uses a combination of written instructions and charts for the knitting. Knitting can be seen in progress in the image, the rounds being tracked with a ruler and pencil. In the image, the green on the chart shows where there are *no* stitches. It can be seen that the knitting is turned inside out to ensure that the yarns do not pull tight during the knitting. The knitting itself is on two circular needles, front stitches on one needle and the back of the hand stitches on the other.

The charts should be followed from bottom to top and from right to left. I suggest that they are photocopied before knitting is started so that progress can be recorded without writing on the book. There are also various sticky notes and tapes available that can be used to do this without damage to the printed page. Knitters may also wish to enlarge the charts before starting to knit. If working from a paper version of the chart, I use a clear ruler and a pencil to mark my progress. If working from a chart on screen I add a marker of another colour at the beginning and end of every round.

Charts are ideal for showing knitting with no shaping, as they are flat, like the knitting they represent. However, when knitting is shaped, as these gloves are, representing the fabric becomes a little tricky. In this picture, the areas in green are those where there is no knitting. At the top of a green area, a stitch is made and then the knitting is indicated in the appropriate colour. In the chart for Pattern 3, the areas below which increases will take place are indicated with a grey square. There is no stitch there.

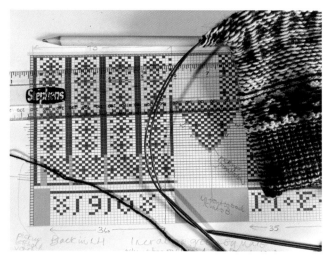

Knitting the M.E.A. glove from a chart.

Pattern 3: Inspired by Mary Allen

Pattern 3: 'Inspired by Mary Allen'.

The pattern for this pair of gloves is inspired by the pair in the Collection of the Knitting & Crochet Guild. They are not an exact replica of the historic ones, but have the characteristic patterns, initials and date of the Yorkshire Dales gloves. Instead, the pattern has been adapted to fit a larger hand, as the originals could not be worn, even by someone with a slim hand as they are extremely narrow and very firmly knitted. They were possibly never worn, but just carried for show.

The yarn specified is spun in Bradford and is 75 per cent wool with 25 per cent polyamide (nylon) meaning that these gloves will stand up to hard wear while being warm. The yarn comes in a wide selection of colours, and although those in this pattern have been knitted in the most common combination of black and cream, Dales gloves have been recorded in red and black and even green and mauve.

Of course, the initials and the date can be customised to suit the intended wearer and charts are given for these in a period style in Appendix II at the end of the book. The choice of the style of the letters and numbers gives either a period or contemporary look.

Materials

Yarn
Cygnet Yarns Ltd Truly Wool Rich 4-ply, 75% Pure New Wool, 25% Polyamide, 50g ball, 205m/224yds.

1 ball Black (Shade 2066), 1 ball Cream (Shade 2614). Finished gloves weigh 76g and take 312m approx.

Needles
2.75mm needles or size to achieve gauge (*see* Chapter 1 for type of knitting needles).

Tools
Stitch markers or lengths of contrasting yarn tied into loops.
Stitch holders and/or lengths of smooth strong contrasting yarn for holding stitches.
Wool sewing needle and scissors for finishing.

Finished size:
To fit a large adult hand.
Length: 28cm/11in.
All round above thumb: 22cm/8.75in.

Tension/gauge:
38 sts x 38 rounds = 10cm/4in square over stocking stitch in two colour pattern knitted in the round.

Abbreviations:
See abbreviations list at back of book.
MC Main colour (Black).
CC Contrast colour (Cream).

Special techniques:
See Chapter 3 'Techniques for knitting two colour gloves', which covers 'casting-on for finger and thumb constructions: various ways'. Two colour cast on instructions given below.
Shaping for finger tips keeps the pattern correct.

Instructions

Right Glove
Cast on using 2 colour long tail (thumb cast-on), as follows. With a slip knot, join both yarns and place on right needle. Wrap white round thumb and use black to knit with, pulling each stitch tight. This forms a black stitch on the needle with white thread below.

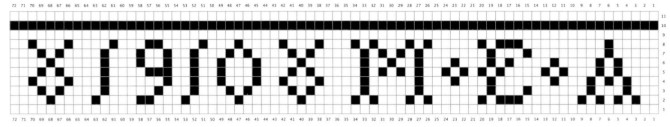

Wrist chart.

Cuff

CO 72 sts using 2 colour cast-on. Join for working in the round. PM for start of round if wanted, checking sts are not twisted.

Round 1: K1 in MC, P1 in CC around.

Work round 1 for a total of 16 rounds.

Next round: K1 in MC, K1 in CC around.

Reading chart from right to left, changing colours where indicated, work from wrist chart rounds 1–11. Adapt initials and date as wished.

Right hand

Reading chart from right to left, changing colours where indicated, and increasing by knitting into the stitch below where indicated, work from right hand chart rounds 1–28.

Round 29: form thumb.

Keeping the pattern correct, K44 sts across back of hand, put 23 sts from thumb onto a length of contrast yarn, CO 8 sts, K35 across palm; 87 sts.

Work rounds 30–46 from Right Hand chart.

Fingers

NOTE: 'Midge and flea' pattern can be continued up the fingers, as photographed, or they can be worked in 'speckle stitch', that is alternating black and white stitches omitting the 'flea'.

Fourth finger:

Break yarns. Put 77 hand sts on length of contrast yarn, keeping pattern correct, K10 sts from palm of hand, K first 11 sts from back of hand on length of yarn, CO 4 sts; 25 sts. Working in the round, keeping pattern correct, knit until finger measures 5.5cm/2.25in, or length required.

Shape the tip:

Round 1: Keeping pattern correct (K3tog, K1) 6 times, K1. 12 sts dec; 13 sts.

Round 2: Keeping pattern correct (K3tog, K1) 3 times, K1. 6 sts dec; 7 sts.

Break yarns, thread yarn needle with MC and thread though the remaining sts. Pull tight and fasten off securely. Take yarn ends to inside of finger.

Third finger:

Keeping pattern correct, K11 sts from palm of hand, PUK 3 from base of fourth finger, K11 from front of hand, CO 4; 29 sts.

Working in the round, keeping pattern correct, knit until finger measures 7cm/2.75in, or length required.

Shape tip:

Round 1: Keeping pattern correct (K3tog, K1) 7 times, K1. 14 sts dec; 15 sts.

Round 2: Keeping pattern correct, (K3tog, K1) 3 times, K3tog. 8 sts dec; 7 sts.

Break yarns, thread yarn needle with MC and thread though the remaining sts. Pull tight and fasten off securely. Take yarn ends to inside of finger.

Second finger:

Keeping pattern correct, K 11 sts from palm of hand, PUK 3 from base of third finger, K11 from front of hand, CO 4; 29 sts.

Working in the round, keeping pattern correct, knit until finger measures 7.5cm/3in, or length required.

Shape tip as third finger.

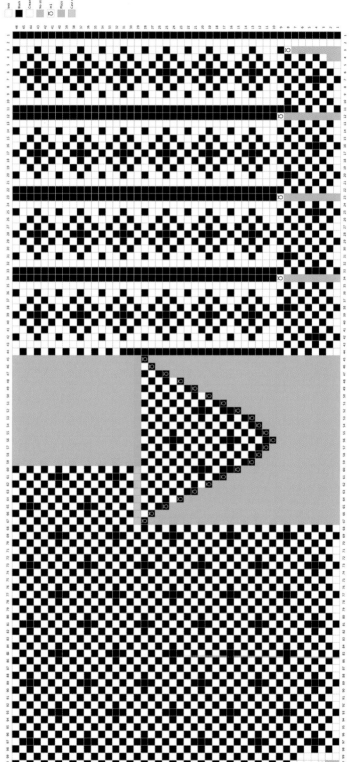

Right hand chart.

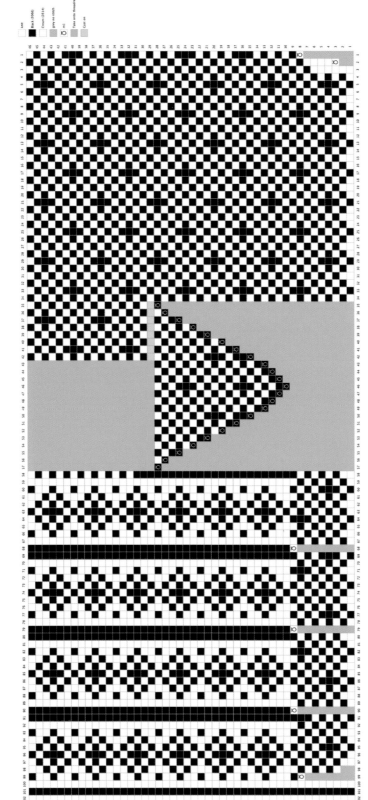

Left hand chart.

First finger:

Keeping pattern correct, K11 sts from palm of hand, PUK 5 from base of second finger, K11 from front of hand; 27 sts.

Working in the round, keeping pattern correct, knit until finger measures 7cm/2.75in, or length required.

Shape the tip:

Round 1: Keeping pattern correct (K3tog, K1) 6 times, K3tog. 14 sts dec; 13 sts.

Round 2: Keeping pattern correct, (K3tog, K1) 3 times, K3tog. 8 sts dec; 7 sts.

Break yarns, thread yarn needle with MC and thread though the remaining sts. Pull tight and fasten off securely. Take yarn ends to inside of finger.

Thumb:

Keeping pattern correct, K 23 sts from contrast yarn, PUK 8 sts from thumb gusset; 31 sts.

Working in the round, keeping pattern correct, knit until thumb measures 5.5cm/2.25in, or length required.

Shape the tip:

Round 1: Keeping pattern correct (K3tog, K1) 7 times, K3tog. 16 sts dec; 15 sts.

Round 2: Keeping pattern correct, (K3tog, K1) 3 times, K3tog. 8 sts dec; 7 sts.

Break yarns, thread yarn needle with MC and thread though the remaining sts. Pull tight and fasten off securely. Take yarn ends to inside of thumb.

Left Glove

Work as right glove until the end of round 11 of wrist chart.

Reading chart from right to left, changing colours where indicated, and increasing by knitting into the stitch below where indicated, work from left hand chart rounds 1–28.

Round 29: form thumb:

K35 sts across palm of hand, put 23 sts from thumb onto a length of contrast yarn, CO 8 sts, K44 across back of hand; 87 sts.

Work rounds 30–46 from left hand chart, above.

Fourth finger:

Keeping pattern correct, K10 sts from palm of hand, slip 66 sts onto length of spare yarn, CO 4 sts, K11 sts from back of hand; 25 sts.

Complete as right hand fourth finger.

Third finger:

Keeping pattern correct, K11 sts from palm of hand, CO 4, K11 from back of hand, PUK 3 from base of fourth finger; 29 sts.

Complete as right hand third finger.

Second finger:

K 11 sts from palm of hand, CO 4, K11 from front of hand, PUK 3 sts from base of third finger; 29 sts.

Complete as right hand second finger.

First finger:

Keeping pattern correct, K22 sts from contrast yarn, PUK 5 sts from base of second finger; 29 sts.

Complete as right hand first finger.

Thumb:

Work as right hand thumb.

Finishing:

Darn in all ends, closing any gaps at the base of the fingers as necessary. Press the gloves according to the instructions with the yarn.

Sanquhar Gloves

In Chapter 2 we saw that Sanquhar is located in Nithsdale, Scotland. Similarly to the Yorkshire Dales, it is an upland area of the UK with agriculture that concentrates on stock rearing and raising sheep. The hills can be seen from the town centre. Knitting, along with weaving and the manufacture of carpets, was carried out in the area. So, let's look more closely at Sanquhar gloves and their continued production there.

What is a Sanquhar Glove?

Sanquhar gloves are noticeably related to Yorkshire Dales, or Dent gloves. They are perhaps not a brother or sister, but are definitely a part of the same family. To mistake a Sanquhar glove for a Yorkshire Dales glove is easily done and completely understandable. The link, if there is any – and it does seem more than coincidental that two types of textiles so unusual and so distinct are found in two separate places – will never be known with any certainty, if at all.

However, Dent and Sanquhar are only just over 100 miles apart overland, and might well have had links between them in the past, although these were never formally documented. Cattle trading might have taken place between the areas, or movement of other livestock, as both the Yorkshire Dales and Nithsdale, where Sanquhar is located, are rural areas. Both cattle rearing and lead mining were carried out in the two places, or near to them. The lead miners were known to move to wherever work was available, and it was common practice to take their families with them when moving for work. Might it be that through these links – livestock and lead mining – knitting was also taken and seen as people moved from one area to the other?

The following characteristics are common to both Dales and Sanquhar gloves: they are knitted in only two colours; they are knitted in the round; and they are knitted in fine yarn, usually wool or a wool-rich mix – this is most often smooth worsted spun yarn, which gives a crisp stitch definition. Both Dales and Sanquhar gloves have the initials of the owner round the wrist, and some Dales gloves have the date too. Both types of glove are patterned with all-over small geometric patterns, and both are the product of skilled knitters. The thumbs are constructed with a gusset, although there is more shaping at the base of the fingers in Sanquhar gloves, especially the Duke pattern, which has small triangular inserts at the finger bases, or finger gussets.

What makes the Sanquhar glove different from the Dales glove? The most often found Sanquhar pattern has a pronounced grid delineating it. This is the Duke, the

The hills from the centre of Sanquhar.

Yorkshire Dales glove and Sanquhar glove, both from the Knitting & Crochet Guild collection.

Sanquhar gloves from the collection of the Knitting & Crochet Guild.

May MacCormick's display of Sanquhar gloves. (Courtesy of May MacCormick)

best known and most commonly knitted of the Sanquhar patterns. The Sanquhar gloves illustrated are in the Duke pattern, and are in the collection of the Knitting & Crochet Guild (KCG). All have been customized with initials at the wrist, and were most likely subsequently donated by a relative of the owner. They perhaps date from the 1960s and 1970s.

There are several variations of pattern in Sanquhar gloves, whereas Dales gloves, or certainly those extant,

have just one variation (of which there are three in total) in the pattern that runs up the back of the hand. Sanquhar gloves have several patterns, each distinct from the others: the Duke, which itself has several variations; the Midge and the Flea or Fly; the Prince of Wales; and the Shepherd's Plaid – and there are others, such as the Pheasant's Eye, the Fleur de Lys, and some that are unnamed, which are perhaps not seen so often. Many of these can be seen in the display, pictured.

On the hands of the Midge and Fly, Prince of Wales and Shepherd's Plaid patterns, three vertical stripes are knitted up the back of the hands, which imitate the hand-stitched seams that are found on good quality leather gloves.

But first, let's look at a Sanquhar glove in a little more detail.

So, what are these special Sanquhar features? Let's take a vintage glove in the Duke pattern, with its distinctive grid. Firstly, there's the cuff, often in corrugated rib, although there are variations, knitted in knit and purl in the two colours of the glove. Above that is the band into which is knitted the initials of the owner, sometimes a whole name, and on occasion 'Sanquhar'. Then the increasing for the thumb begins to accommodate two whole-pattern squares. The hands are neatly laid out with squares containing alternating patterns, the most usual 'fillings' being diamonds.

When the fingers are started, the construction includes a triangular gusset, which is then decreased to form the vertical edge of the grid. These finger gussets, or fourchettes, are unusual in contemporary hand-knitted gloves, although they are frequently found in historic examples, especially finely knitted liturgical gloves. The tips of the fingers are decreased in a way that preserves the continuity of the vertical grid lines.

And of course there are variations. Cuffs can include single stitches breaking up the pattern; in fact, there are many variations even in the cuff or ribbing. In the pattern for the Shepherd's Plaid there is a contrasting lining knitted in the cuff, so that it is double and the cuff is knitted in stocking stitch. The most commonly knitted Sanquhar pattern in recent years has been the Duke, with diamonds inside the grid squares. This can be varied by using different patterns within the gridlines, or dambrod, as in the patterns published and available in the town, mentioned above. There is a large choice from those traditionally used in

A vintage Sanquhar glove with pleated fingers.

Thumb gusset from the vintage Sanquhar glove.

Finger gusset in the vintage Sanquhar glove.

Cuff of the vintage Sanquhar glove.

Vintage Sanquhar glove fingertips.

A variety of Sanquhar glove cuffs.

The Southern Upland Way goes through the centre of Sanquhar.

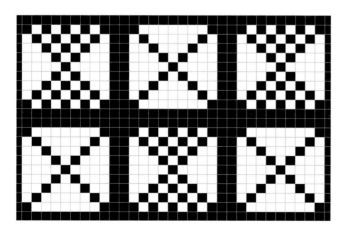

Chart for Cornet's pattern.

Sanquhar to those designed to more individual tastes. Contemporary designer knitters have varied the pattern with mathematical symbols and other patterns, of which more are shown in Chapter 4.

Sanquhar gloves are still being knitted in the town well into the twenty-first century, while it is thought that the last glove knitter in the Yorkshire Dales, Mary Allen, died in 1924. What are the reasons that gloves are still knitted by hand in Sanquhar? And why were they knitted there in the first place? These are questions that have been explored by textile historians and designers with some interesting results.

In attempting to answer these questions, Sanquhar itself has to be visited, at least in the imagination. Sanquhar is reached by road or rail through the countryside of southern Scotland. The hills of the Southern Uplands rise around it, and the long-distance hiking trail, the Southern Upland Way, goes through the small town.

Various events and people have contributed to the promotion of the Sanquhar glove since its emergence in the nineteenth century, mentioned in Chapter 2. In common with other small towns in southern Scotland, Sanquhar has an annual ceremony known as the 'Riding of the Marches', in which local people on horseback trace the town's boundaries. In recent times this has taken place in Sanquhar since 1910. According to information in May MacCormick's leaflet for Cornet pattern gloves, in 1937 there was a revival, and from this time, the three 'principals' who lead the horseback procession are each presented with a pair of Sanquhar gloves. The Cornet has a pair in the Cornet pattern, and the other principals have gloves in the Duke pattern.

A further part of the Sanquhar jigsaw, which might be an important factor in the continuation of the knitting of the gloves, and almost as complicated as the construction of the gloves themselves, is a teacher at the local academy or secondary school. Mary Forsyth, from Sanquhar, born in 1910, left the town to train as a teacher, and then returned in 1933 to teach at Sanquhar Academy, where her subject was home economics. Under her regime, every girl in the school knitted a pair of Sanquhar gloves during their time there. In addition to the local girls learning the skill, girls from a school in Glasgow were evacuated to Sanquhar during World War II and became familiar with the Sanquhar glove, and took this knowledge back to Glasgow, spreading it further. Mary Forsyth died in 2001, but her legacy in the form of the continuation of the knitting of gloves in Sanquhar carries on.

Mary Forsyth, from a Sanquhar Academy staff photo, 1970. (Image courtesy of William Dalgleish, Sanquhar)

The long tradition of knitting Sanquhar gloves for visitors continued throughout the twentieth century. Sanquhar gloves could be ordered at a small shop in the town and would be ready for the purchaser within a week – that is, before they went back home after their holiday in the town. They are still for sale in the local arts centre, A' The Airts. However, knowledge of how to knit them became more widespread with the publication of printed patterns.

At this time in the UK, two trends in wider society occurred, which again, fortuitously, enabled the continuance of the Sanquhar knitting tradition. Following World War II, 1939–45, women who had been in the Forces, or who had been employed in essential war work, were expected to return to their more accustomed pre-war roles as housewives and mothers. The market for women's magazines boomed, as this population was educated and informed about home-making activities.

Alongside this, interest in both national and international travel was growing, with a rise in prosperity. Fashion trends, including those for hand knitting, looked to 'traditional' knits for inspiration, including those in places such as Scandinavia and Latvia. What has this got to do with knitted gloves from a small town in rural Scotland? These trends perhaps ensured the first

step in the perpetuation of Sanquhar knitting: that of writing down the patterns for publication and wider distribution.

Patterns for Sanquhar Gloves

One publisher of these patterns for garments inspired by traditional or folk or ethnic knitting was the UK firm of Patons & Baldwins. Part of a series of leaflets that included knits from Shetland and Latvia, their pattern for Sanquhar gloves was published in 1954. Entitled *Sanquhar Gloves, A Traditional Scottish Style* on the cover of the leaflet, inside the heading reads 'Sanquhar in Dumfriesshire gives its name to these traditional gloves'.

A women's magazine, *The People's Friend*, published in the Scottish town of Dundee, presented two special knitting supplements in the mid-1950s, for Scottish knitting and Sanquhar knitting. Both these booklets gave patterns for Sanquhar knitwear in the form of glove and scarf sets, the second one adding a woman's twinset, a child's cap and boys' knee-length socks specifically in the Sanquhar pattern.

Patons and Baldwins leaflet 87 for Sanquhar gloves.

Pattern booklets given with The People's Friend *magazine.*

These publications and patterns, especially those given in widely read women's magazines, helped to ensure that the knowledge of Sanquhar knitting was disseminated.

Following this, in the 1960s the Scottish Rural Women's Institute (SWRI, now re-named as the Scottish Women's Institute), recorded and published instructions for making Sanquhar gloves. The Midge and Fly pattern was the first to be issued in 1966, and the leaflet gave a little of the history of the Sanquhar glove knitting too, stating: 'For two centuries at least, this craft has passed from generation to generation in the small town of Sanquhar in Dumfriesshire ....' This bit of history goes on to say that the gloves were 'originally knitted in drugget on fine needles'. Drugget, a type of yarn, is thought to have been a mix of wool and cotton or flax that was obtained from the local carpet factory in the neighbouring village of Crawick; it would have been very hardwearing and also crisp in appearance – in other words, ideal for the knitting of finely patterned gloves.

The SWRI published three further patterns for the Duke, Shepherd's Plaid and Prince of Wales designs through the 1970s, with the last appearing in about 1980. None of these leaflets includes charts for the knitting, but they give line-by-line instructions for the two-colour patterning. These were reformatted and issued again in the mid-2010s, but again without charts for the patterned knitting.

Now, in the twenty-first century, pattern booklets for Sanquhar Duke pattern gloves and Sanquhar stockings were designed and published by Alison Thomson, who came to Sanquhar with her husband when he became the minister there. Her glove booklet giving full instructions and charts for the Duke pattern is dated 2009. She also encouraged the production of machine-knitted garments in the Sanquhar patterns. This activity has been continued by Sanquhar Pattern Designs in premises next door to the arts centre, where a range of 'Sanquhar' pattern garments are available (*see* Resources section at the back of this book).

May MacCormick, whose display of gloves was shown earlier, learnt how to knit Sanquhar gloves from her mother, and also studied the gloves knitted by another Sanquhar teacher, Miss Jane Forsyth (no relation to Mary Forsyth). May and her gloves were selected to be shown at the Smithsonian Folklife Festival, Washington DC, USA, in 2003 as part of the Scotland exhibit there. May is an authority on the glove knitting of Sanquhar, and is in the process of recording and publishing patterns for all the different Sanquhar patterns, some of which are shown. She gives classes on Sanquhar glove knitting, and also takes part in the Sanquhar Knitting Tours organized by A' The Airts.

There are nine leaflets for variations on the Duke pattern, based on the square or dambrod, and several other variations, including a hat pattern and one for children's gloves and mittens. These patterns are sold in the shop that sells the knitting yarns in the town of Sanquhar itself, and in the arts centre (*see* Resources).

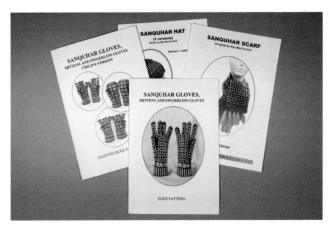

Leaflets for Sanquhar patterns by May MacCormick.

All these different elements have contributed to the continued existence of the Sanquhar glove, from its roots in the availability of wool and textile manufacture, with knitting being part of local activities, to the support of the local landowner in the late nineteenth century. The use of the gloves in an annual ceremony, the Riding of the Marches, gave the gloves prominence, and the preservation of the knitting skills passed to schoolgirls from both Sanquhar and Glasgow spread the skill and knowledge of their making.

The recording of the instructions for knitting the various patterns of Sanquhar gloves, by knitting yarn manufacturers, publishers and social organizations, has ensured that it is possible for anyone with an interest to knit a pair. Add to this the difficulty of knitting a true Sanquhar glove by machine, or certainly not one with the features of a hand-knitted one, and the continuation of their making is assured. Classes are being held in the town to pass on the skills needed to knit them, while there are Sanquhar knitting groups on the internet, interest being high in the USA and Canada (*see* Resources).

The Tolbooth Museum in the centre of the town has displays giving the history of Sanquhar gloves and many examples of them; it is open in the summer months, and has other displays of local history. Gloves and other items in the range of Sanquhar patterns are available for sale in the arts centre, shop and café, called 'A' The Airts', just over the road from the Tolbooth Museum, as well as pattern leaflets. Wool, needles and pattern leaflets are sold in the craft shop over the road (*see* Resources).

A' The Airts, Sanquhar.

Tools and Materials for Knitting Sanquhar Gloves

Each knitter will have a preference for the type of knitting needles chosen for this project, as discussed in Chapter 1.

Yarn for a 'traditional' Sanquhar glove, such as a pure wool or wool/polyamide mix of a suitable fineness, has become harder to source. However, a wool mix yarn sold as 'Sanquhar 3-ply' is available on-line, in black or white only (*see* Resources). Some lighter '4-ply' (UK) or 'fingering' (USA) can work, but it is vital to check the tension/gauge before

The Tolbooth Museum, Sanquhar.

Tools and materials for Sanquhar gloves.

starting out, as it is not possible to adjust for size due to the geometry of the patterns. Both vintage 3-ply pure wool and sock wool work well, but have to be sourced from the internet. It is worth trying different size needles to achieve a suitable fabric for the size of glove wanted.

Patterns for Sanquhar Gloves

Patterns for Sanquhar gloves can be obtained from several sources, both electronic and through the post. Vintage patterns may also be bought on the internet, although availability varies.

The Patons and Baldwins pattern leaflet 87 can be obtained from the Knitting & Crochet Guild through their website (*see* Resources). This is available for both Guild members and non-members.

Warning: As specified, the glove knits up very small. To fit an adult hand, this pattern has to be knitted on a larger needle with thicker yarn.
The Scottish Women's Institute publishes patterns that can be ordered through its website (*see* Resources).

'Ravelry', the website for knitters, also has examples of Sanquhar glove patterns.

There are patterns for Sanquhar gloves on the internet, usually given as diagrams. These are relatively easy to follow for the knitter familiar with using charted knitting designs. Stitch numbers are given, and patterns charted enabling the glove to be constructed accordingly.

The most recent patterns published, and the ones sold in Sanquhar itself, mentioned earlier, are those recorded by May MacCormick, who has been knitting these gloves all her adult life. Her patterns can be obtained through the post from the arts centre or the craft shop in Sanquhar (*see* Resources).

However, those of May MacCormick might be regarded as 'definitive', as she says in the introduction and history of each pattern.

Pattern 4: Inspired by Alba

Pattern 4: 'Inspired by Alba'.

This pattern has been designed as an easy entry into two colour glove knitting. If worked with the recommended tweedy yarn or a similar one, any inconsistencies in the knitting will be forgiven. The Milarrochy Tweed yarn from Kate Davies Designs, contains 30 per cent mohair blended with the wool adding strength and durability and making it ideal for gloves. The pattern on the hand is constructed from alternate rounds of knit 3 main colour and knit 3 contrast colour, with rounds of alternating single stitches to build the small checks.

The fingers are knitted in a pattern of alternate stitches that change on the following round to make a tiny checkerboard. It is sometimes called seed stitch, but this is easy to confuse with textured patterns like moss stitch. In this pattern it is called 'speckle' pattern. The start of the little finger is not dropped in this pattern, making it simpler in construction and both hands are the same.

Materials

Yarns:
Kate Davies Designs, Milarrochy Tweed, 70% wool 30% mohair, 4ply/fingering, 25g/100m/109yds, MC (Bruce), 2 x 25g balls, CC (Cranachan), 2 x 25g balls. Finished gloves weigh 52g and take 108m approx.

Needles
3.25mm knitting needles or size to achieve gauge (*see* Chapter 1 for type of knitting needles).

Tools
Stitch markers or lengths of contrasting yarn tied into loops. Stitch holders and/or lengths of smooth strong contrasting yarn for holding stitches.
Wool sewing needle and scissors for finishing.

Finished size:
Length 25cm/9.75in long, 18cm/7in all-round above thumb.

Tension/gauge:
36 sts and 36 rounds = 10cm/4in square over two-colour pattern knitted in the round.

Abbreviations:
See abbreviations list at back of book.
Main colour MC.
Contrast colour CC.

Special techniques:
See Chapter 3 'Techniques for knitting in two colours', which covers 'casting on for finger and thumb constructions: various ways'.

Instructions

Note: Both gloves are the same.
Speckle stitch is alternate colours in stitches and rounds as in the 7 rounds above the rib.

Cuff:
CO 60 sts using MC. Join for working in the round. PM for start of round if wanted, checking sts are not twisted.
In MC work 1 round in K2 P2 rib.
Next round: 2 colour rib: K2 MC, P2 CC, rep to end of round.
Repeat this round 13 times; 14 rounds in 2 colour rib (*see* chart rounds 2–15).

Knit 1 round in MC, increasing 1 st (M1L) at beginning of round: 61 sts.

Reading chart from right to left, changing colours where indicated, work from chart rounds 17–23.

Thumb shaping:
Following hand and thumb charts, changing colours and increasing sts as indicated.
Chart round 24: In MC, K31sts, PM, M1L, PM, K31sts. Thumb gusset is now set up between markers.
Chart rounds 25–46: Work from hand and thumb charts as set, increasing either side of thumb gusset as indicated on chart; 84 sts.
Chart round 47: form thumb:
Work 32 sts in pattern, put 21 thumb sts onto length of contrast yarn, remove markers, CO 3 sts, work 31 sts in pattern to end of round; 66 sts.
Chart round 48: Work from hand chart as set to end of round.

Following hand chart and changing colours, work chart rounds 49–64 or to length required to base of fingers.

Work the Fingers
Break yarns. Place first st of round, the MC 'seam' st, on to a length of contrast yarn with the 23 sts to both right and left of it; 47 sts total. 19 sts on needles.

First finger:
Re-join yarns and knit these 19 sts in speckle pattern, (alternate MC and CC sts), CO 6 sts using MC and CC alternately, 25 sts. Working in the round, keeping pattern correct, knit until finger measures 6.5cm/2.5 in or about 0.5cm/0.25in short of length required.

Shape the tip:
Round 1: Keeping pattern correct (K3tog, K1), 6 times, K1; 12 sts dec; 13 sts.
Round 2: Keeping pattern correct, (K3tog, K1), 3 times, K1; 6 sts dec; 7 sts.
Break yarns, thread yarn needle with MC and thread though the remaining sts. Pull tight and fasten off securely. Take yarn ends to inside of finger.

Key
knit   MC (Buurå)   CC (Cainachan)   Grey no stitch   purl   M1R   M1L   Place sts onto thread   Cast-on

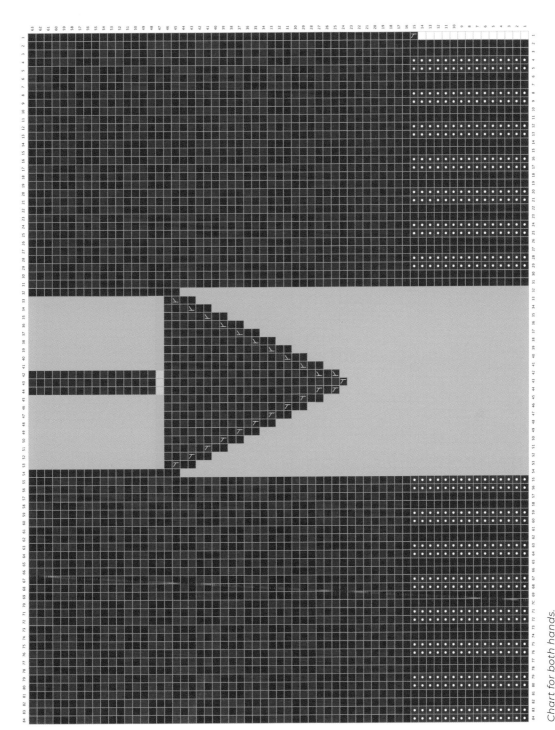

Chart for both hands.

Second finger:

Keeping pattern correct, K8 sts from contrast yarn, using MC and CC yarns alternately PUK 5 sts from the base of the first finger, K8 sts from contrast yarn, CO 4 sts using MC and CC yarn alternately; 25 sts.

Working in the round, keeping pattern correct, knit until finger measures 7.5cm/2.75in or about 0.5cm/0.25in short of length required.

Complete as given for first finger.

Third finger:

Keeping pattern correct, K7 sts from contrast yarn, using MC and CC yarns alternately PUK 5 sts from the base of the second finger, K7 sts from contrast yarn, CO 6 sts using MC and CC yarn alternately; 25 sts.

Working in the round, keeping pattern correct, knit until finger measures 6.5cm/2.5in or about 0.5cm/0.25in short of length required.

Complete as given for first finger.

Fourth finger:

Keeping pattern correct, K17 sts on contrast yarn, using MC and CC yarns alternately PUK 6 sts from base of third finger; 23 sts.

Working in the round, keeping pattern correct, knit until finger measures 5.5cm/2.25in or about 0.5cm/0.25in short of length required.

Shape the tip:

Round 1: Keeping pattern correct (K3tog, k1) 5 times, k3 tog. 12 sts dec; 11 sts.

Round 2: Keeping pattern correct, (k3tog, k1) twice, k3tog. 5 sts.

Finish as given for first finger.

Thumb:

Return to sts on contrast yarn for thumb gusset. Keeping pattern correct, K21 sts from the contrast yarn, using MC and CC yarns alternately PUK6 sts from thumb gusset CO,

join for working in the round; 27 sts. Knit in pattern for 5cm/2in or about 0.5cm/0.25in short of length required.

Shape the tip:

Round 1: Keeping pattern correct (K3tog, k1) 6 times, K3tog. 14 sts dec; 13 sts.

Round 2: Keeping pattern correct, (k3tog, k1) 3 times, K1. 6 sts dec; 7 sts.

Finish as given for first finger.

Knit the second glove to match. As the gloves are symmetrical, there is not a right and a left glove although this preference will become apparent in wear.

Finishing:

Darn in all ends, closing any gaps at the base of the fingers as necessary. Give the gloves a light press with a hot iron and damp cloth or according to instructions given with the yarn.

'Inspired by Alba' gloves – cuff and thumb detail.

Gloves in Estonia

The gloves of the Yorkshire Dales are austere in their limited palette of two colours and their range of three tightly varied patterns.

Sanquhar gloves have several different named patterns with many variations on the most common of these. Black and white are a common choice of colours, but a wide selection of colours is used in their knitting. The cuffs can also vary from glove to glove and knitter to knitter. So Sanquhar gloves can be found in a range of variations around the recognized patterns.

Moving on to Estonia, it is a different prospect altogether. The National Museum in Tartu has many hundreds of pairs of gloves, in fact over three thousand, in its collection, possibly with no two pairs the same. Shops and stalls at specialist fairs offer huge ranges of patterns. Almost every knitting technique known can be found, not to mention every possible colour combination. Regional specialities and island patterns vie for attention. So where to start?

Firstly, a little background about Estonia: its history and geography.

Estonia: Some Context

Estonia is the most northerly of the three Baltic states, the others being Latvia and Lithuania to its south, its location being shown on the map given in Chapter 2. These countries have had chequered histories over the centuries. With the former Soviet Union (USSR) to its east, Estonia has been both an independent state and an occupied territory over the course of many centuries. It declared independence in 1918, only to become part of the USSR after World War II. It became independent of the USSR in 1991 following the collapse of the Eastern bloc, but Cyrillic characters (Russian letters) can still be found on signs and labels, and the influence of the USSR is still apparent in the style of some buildings in both urban and rural areas.

Estonia, Crafts and Culture

For small nations wanting to assert themselves, cultural forms, including literature, music and the visual arts, are important vehicles. Crafts, whether textiles, or making with other materials, can be an integral part of these expressions of nationhood and identity. This is the case in many parts of the world, from Scotland and Wales in the UK to northern Europe in the Scandinavian nations, and further afield in Africa, Asia and Latin America.

Estonian crafts have been part of the means of establishing a national identity both throughout the nineteenth century and since independence from the USSR in 1991. National dress, based on the local area or parish, has been worn since the nineteenth century, often including gloves or mittens as part of these outfits. Other garments knitted in Estonia include hats and socks as well as jackets and sweaters. National dress from the nineteenth century is well represented in the National Museum displays, but is also worn for celebrations and for events for tourists.

Such is the importance of all kinds of cultural activities that they are taught at university level in order both to preserve

Estonian rural scene at Olustvere.

National dress on display in the Estonian National Museum, Tartu. (Courtesy of Kadri Vissel, Estonian National Museum)

Tour guide wearing national dress. (Courtesy of Laura Jõe)

found in the region of Estonia since the late Middle Ages, if only fragments, with the earliest examples of knitted gloves in the National Museum collection dating from the 1790s. Glove knitting carries on today, and it is to this that we now turn.

So, What Does an Estonian Glove Look Like?

Let's take a look at some examples, all drawn from my personal collection and bought in Estonia. With the variety of colours and patterns that are on sale, the difficulty of making a selection can only be imagined!

Estonian Gloves with an Entrelac Cuff

This pair, closely knitted in pure wool and in eight colours, boasts cuffs that are the first thing to catch the eye. The deep cuff is knitted in entrelac, the knitted construction that looks as though the knitting is composed of narrow strips woven together, although this is not how it is knitted. There are eight colours in this cuff, some grading into each other and some providing a 'pop' of bright colour. Both bright pink and orange may be characteristic of Estonian knitting, and

them and to ensure their continuation. The University of Tartu's Department of Native Crafts offers degree and post-graduate courses, which include traditional building, metalwork and textiles. The range of textiles includes fibre preparation, spinning, dyeing, weaving, various types of braiding, embroidery and, of course, knitting.

These crafts are also taught to an international audience through an annual Craft Camp, hosted in the small town of Viljandi, the home of the Native Crafts department. In addition, the Estonian National Museum, housed in an ultra-modern building in Tartu, a city considered to be the cultural capital of Estonia, has large holdings of folk textiles. Smaller regional museums also have impressive collections, while all types of crafts are available to buy in shops in the capital Tallin and other towns and cities.

In this context, hand knitting has an important place in the Estonian cultural scene, and has been documented in books in Estonian about gloves and mittens, and also in a series of three definitive books about Estonian knitting, two of which have been translated into English. Knitting has been

Estonian gloves with an entrelac cuff. (Courtesy of Kristi Jõeste)

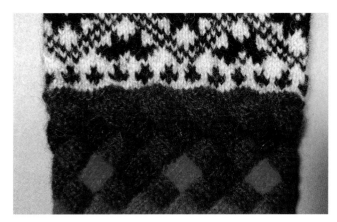

Detail of entrelac glove. (Courtesy of Kristi Jõeste)

these are here. Entrelac is a time-consuming technique to knit, requiring changes of direction of the work and picking up stitches to work the small squares of colour. At this scale, on double-pointed needles smaller than 2mm in size, and in the round, it is skilled and detailed work.

Above the striking cuff, the hand starts with a small geometric pattern in three colours, almost imperceptible and shown in the detailed image, giving way to a larger diamond and star pattern on the back and palms of the hand in a dark navy and light grey. These colours are also used for the fingers and thumb, which are knitted in yet another pattern of smaller geometric figures. The thumb is a peasant thumb (*see* Chapter 1 for thumb constructions) set into the palm of the hand, and the fourth finger, the little finger, is set lower down in the hand to give a better fit.

The glove is knitted in pure wool and has an almost felted appearance as it will have been washed after the knitting was completed. The tension or gauge of the knitting is fine: about 50 stitches per 10cm (12 stitches per 1in). The gloves are 25cm (9.75in) long, to fit an adult hand.

Although looking very modern, there is a glove in the National Museum with an entrelac cuff that is dated 1841, and many more examples from the following years.

This glove is from the workshop of Kristi Jõeste, an Estonian designer, teacher and knitter who has made extensive studies of historic gloves in Estonia, studying them by reproducing them. Her book about Estonian gloves, *Ornamented Journey*, is a lovely combination of photographs of her work, with stories and poetry by another Estonian writer, Kristiina Ehin. Kristi is also one of the authors of the first book in a series of three about Estonian knitting, *Estonian Knitting 1: Traditions and Techniques*, published by the Estonian publishing house, Saara books; it is available in English, as is *Ornamented Journey* (*see* Bibliography).

Gloves with Sideways Knitted Cuffs

The second pair of Estonian gloves contrasts with the first pair, being brightly coloured (*see* photograph); three different greens are the background for small patterns in yellow and purple pure wool. The cuff of this pair is knitted sideways in wedges of garter stitch using a short row technique, and joined into a round, giving it a decidedly contemporary look. However, this cuff structure can be found on a pair dating from the early twentieth century (1909) in the National Museum collection (also pictured).

This pair, over a hundred years old, ERM 18523ab, has a modern feel with its black hands and multicoloured patterning, despite having been worn quite a lot! These are identified as coming from Setomaa, a remote area in the east of Estonia. The sideways garter stitch, short row cuff is also found on mittens from Latvia, so is found elsewhere.

Returning to the contemporary pair, above this crisp cuff, the knitting progresses up the hand and fingers in small geometric patterns. These continue into the fingers using each contrast colour in turn so that each finger has a different colour set against the bright green background. The thumb is again a peasant thumb, allowing the pattern to continue uninterrupted from the hand up the thumb. The fourth (little) finger begins lower on the hand, meaning that the colour pattern does not repeat across the hand.

Estonian gloves with sideways knitted cuffs. (Courtesy of Külli Jacobson)

Gloves dated 1909 from the National Museum, ERM 18523ab. (Creative Commons licence)

A colourful show of hand-knitted gloves for sale in Estonia. (Courtesy of Külli Jacobson)

This glove is also knitted in pure wool with a tension or gauge of about 40 stitches to 10cm (10 stitches to 1in), giving a very firm fabric, warm and hard wearing.

The glove is one of those hand knitted by the company Nordic Knitters, run by Külli Jacobson, with a huge variety of hand-knitted gloves and mittens, a tiny selection of which can be seen in the image showing a display of gloves from the company. Külli also organizes craft visits to Estonia, and teaches knitting from her home in the south-east of the country.

Gloves from the Island of Saaremaa, Estonia

There is much to interest the knitter in this third pair of Estonian gloves shown. It has garter-stitch bands edging the top and bottom edges of the cuff, increases and decreases forming a structured scalloped lower edge, and two-colour patterns on the hand and palm. In three colours of pure wool, it is a classic example of a glove from the large island of Saaremaa in the Baltic to the west of the Estonian mainland.

The patterns on the back of the hands are matched across the fingers so that the pattern appears to be continuous when the gloves are laid flat with the back of the hands upwards. On the palm side of the gloves, from above the base of the thumb, the two-colour diamond pattern changes to a pattern of vertical stripes, which then continues up the palm side of the fingers.

The thumb has the outward facing side in the diamond pattern but the palm-facing side has the vertical pattern giving a small, but attractive, visual surprise (illustrated). The fourth finger is lower in its start than the others, but this difference is almost invisible due to the clever construction. This glove is worked in heavier wool than the first two, giving about 36 stitches to 10cm (9 stitches to 1in). The fabric is more open than that of the previous two pairs, making the gloves more flexible and perhaps more comfortable to wear. This glove is from the workshop of Riina Tomberg, a well-known Estonian designer, teacher, textile historian and expert knitter.

Gloves from Saaremaa, Estonia. (Courtesy of Riina Tomberg)

Detail of the thumb of a Saaremaa glove. (Courtesy of Riina Tomberg)

Glove from Mustjala parish in the collection of the Estonian National Museum ERM_5138. (Creative Commons licence)

This design was adapted by Riina from one in the National Collection, ERM_5138, from the parish of Mustjala on Saaremaa. One of the foremost experts in all kinds of Estonian knitting, Riina says the pattern had to be adapted to use twenty-four stitches fewer around the hand, 'without losing the character of the glove'.

Between them, these gloves demonstrate many features common to Estonian gloves, although perhaps not all that are to be found in the over three thousand pairs in the National Museum collection!

In Summary: Features of a 'Typical' Estonian Glove

Knitted in wool: Many Estonian woven textiles are made in cotton and linen; however, this is not the case for gloves or mittens that are needed to keep hands warm. As with all knitting historically, the wool for Estonian knitting was originally from local sheep. Locally sourced wool is still available that is designed for knitting gloves and mittens in the traditional way. However beware: the thickness of Estonian wools is described using the count system, as in the textile industry, in which the number of component threads in the yarn are paired with their thickness using a length and weight measurement. Thus an 8/2 has two threads plied together, while an 8/1 is a single thread.

A firm fabric: Estonian knitting usually has a very high gauge or tension, using fine needles to produce a firm fabric. As with so many textiles from any part of the world, from patchwork to embroidery, older work is often finer, reflecting lives when more time was available for hand manufacture. Older pieces are more likely to have been made for the personal use of the knitter or their family, rather than for sale, and were therefore more finely knitted. Some of the examples in the National Museum have over 100 stitches round the cuff, while those shown here have between sixty-four and ninety-six stitches around it.

Includes pattern: Pattern, in the form of colourwork or texture, sometimes both, is an almost universal feature of hand-knitted Estonian gloves. Sometimes embroidery is added after knitting, and also fringes, if they have not been knitted in. The title of Kristi Jõeste's book about Estonian gloves, *Ornamented Journey*, is very appropriate.

Uses a peasant thumb: The peasant thumb is the most commonly found construction for the thumb. This has several advantages in that it allows the pattern of the hand to continue without the interruption of the thumb gusset, and its position can be altered with ease.

Knitted in the round: Estonian gloves are always knitted in the round, using a set of five double-pointed needles, the stitches on four being knitted with the fifth.

Washed: The knitting is washed after completion and is slightly fulled or felted, thus ensuring maximum warmth and hardwearing qualities.

Techniques Used in Estonian Glove Knitting

The techniques used in knitting Estonian gloves are very numerous, as can be seen even from the small selection already shown. Perhaps the key feature of Estonian knitting is the firmness of the fabric, in other words the high number of stitches to the centimetre or inch. This is achieved by knitting with fine needles and relatively heavier wool, giving a very close fabric. It is closed up even more when the work is washed after completion and any residual oil in the wool removed.

Knitting in the Round Using Five Needles

When knitting in the round Estonian knitters use double-pointed needles in sets of five. The basic unit of the pattern is the needle, and instructions are most often given in terms of each needle. So instead of saying 'cast on 80 stitches', the instruction will be 'cast on 20 stitches on each needle'. Estonian knitting on four needles is pictured in Chapter 1.

Colours and Colourwork

A glove without any colourwork is rare in Estonia. Many have colourwork all over, whether stranded in two or three colours in the round, or manipulated in techniques such as entrelac. There are also inlay techniques, sometimes known as *roositud*, in which a separate length of yarn is incorporated into the knitted fabric giving striking patterns. Intarsia is worked to form motifs on the back of the hands, while colourwork can be found in cuff patterns, as already seen.

Historically, as in other places, contrast in knitting was achieved by using the natural colours of light and dark sheep's wool. Wool was also dyed with local plants to give yellows, blues and reds, to the extent that whole islands were denuded of that vegetation! Like many craftspeople, Estonian knitters embraced the bright colours available with the coming of chemical dyes, this being taken to striking lengths by the knitters on Muhu Island, who have used the combination of orange and pink as one of their signature features.

Other colour combinations are characteristic of particular islands. Cream with navy is a hallmark of knitting from Ruhnu Island, while the island of Kuhnu typically features cream with navy and a deep red.

Most often, Estonian yarns are dyed with solid colours, but early examples of tie-dyed and space-dyed yarns appear, the earliest in the National Museum being from 1851; these

Glove from Muhu Island with typical colours of orange and pink ERM_14226-a. (Creative Commons licence)

Gloves with random yarn ERM A 509. 2855. (Creative Commons licence)

Lace gloves on display for sale in Estonia.

are followed by others from the early twentieth century, giving them a contemporary look that would not be out of place in a twenty-first-century knitter's bag.

The Cuffs

As we have seen on the three Estonian gloves examined in detail earlier, highly patterned cuffs are an extremely common feature in many, if not the majority of Estonian gloves. These patterns can be lace, travelling stitches, combinations of eyelets and garter-stitch ridges, braids, embroidery and fringes. A rib that might be considered standard in other places is rarely seen, and when it is, it is likely to be striped or two coloured! A further variation is a rib that is shaped so that it forms diagonals, similar to the entrelac, actually known as 'faux entrelac'. This construction requires increasing and decreasing at almost every stitch on every round, and is therefore hard work for the knitter.

Gloves are knitted in lace patterns, which are sometimes used for the whole glove, but often just for part of it.

Travelling stitches such as twisted stitches are often found in white gloves. These sometimes have some contrast colour in the cuff and are extremely striking, especially when knitted in white or cream and a dark indigo navy blue. The selection shown here, from the 'Estonian White' exhibition in Viljandi, Estonia, in 2018 includes gloves and wrist warmers, some with over 100 stitches round the wrist. They were knitted by Anu Pink and Siiri Reimann for the exhibition.

This is just a tiny insight into the gloves of Estonia, a source of wonder to all knitters and a testimony to the skill and endless creativity of their makers over at least two hundred years.

Reproduction of a fringed wedding glove from Karja, Estonia, knitted by Kristi Jõeste. (Courtesy of Kristi Jõeste)

Gloves and fingerless mitts from Ruhnu Island knitted by Anu Pink and Siiri Reimann for the 'Estonian White' exhibition 2018.

Pattern 5: Boreal Inspiration

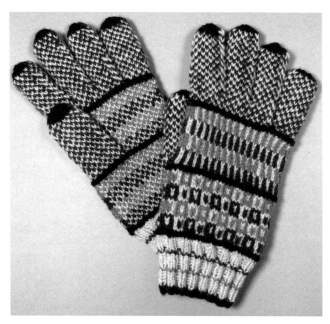

Pattern 5: 'Boreal Inspiration'.

This pair is in the tradition of the patterned gloves from cold places in the world, from Estonia and the Baltic, to Scandinavia, the UK and Canada. Knitted in a pure wool double knitting weight from Shetland, with a simple peasant thumb, these gloves might make a good introduction to patterned knitting. Knitted as specified, the fabric is dense and warm. The pattern could be varied with a lighter yarn, thicker needles or different colours. The palm and fingers are knitted in speckle pattern, that is alternate colour stitches every round.

Materials

Yarn
Jamieson of Shetland, Double Knitting, 100% wool, 25g balls/75m, 2 balls in main colour, MC (Eggshell 768), 1 ball each in 3 contrast colours CC1 (Dark Navy 730), CC2 (Pumpkin 470), CC3 (Cobalt 684).
Finished gloves weigh 84g and take 252m/276 yds approx.

Needles
3.75mm knitting needles or size to achieve gauge (*see* earlier in Chapter 1 for type of knitting needles).
3.25mm needles for the rib, if preferred but not essential.

Tools
Stitch markers or lengths of contrasting yarn tied into loops.
Length of contrasting yarn of the same weight for knitting stitches for thumb opening.
Stitch holders and/or lengths of smooth strong contrasting yarn for holding stitches.
Wool sewing needle and scissors for finishing.

Finished size:
To fit a large adult hand.
Length: 26cm/10.25in.
Width above thumb: 11cm/4.25in.

Tension/gauge:
30 sts x 32 rounds = 10cm/4in square over two-colour pattern knitted in the round, after light steam.

Abbreviations:
See abbreviations list at back of book.
MC Main colour (Eggshell 768).
CC1 Contrast colour 1 (Dark Navy 730)
CC2 Contrast colour 2 (Pumpkin 470).
CC3 Contrast colour 3 (Cobalt 684).

Special techniques:
See Chapter 3 'Techniques for knitting in two colours. *See also* Chapter 1', which covers 'casting-on for finger and thumb constructions: various ways'.

Instructions

Right glove
Using CC1 CO 60 sts on 3.25 or 3.75mm needles as preferred.
Join for working in the round.
Place marker for start of round if wanted, checking sts are not twisted.
Work 1 round in K2, p2 rib.

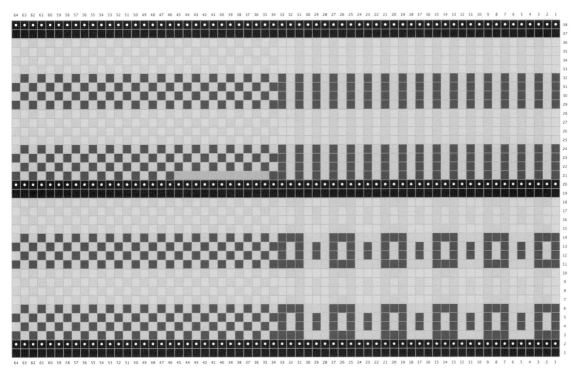

Right hand Boreal chart.

Join MC work 5 rounds in K2, P2 rib.

Join CC2 work 1 round in K2, P2 rib.

Using MC work 5 rounds in K2, P2 rib.

Join CC3 work 1 round in K2, P2 rib.

Using MC work 5 rounds in K2, P2 rib.

Change to 3.75 needles if necessary.

K1 round increasing as follows: (K15, M1L) 4 times. 4 sts inc; 64 sts*

Reading chart from right to left, changing colours where indicated, work from Right glove chart rounds 1–20.

NB rounds 2, 20 and 38 are purled.

Place thumb:

Next round (chart round 21): Keeping pattern correct, K34, using length of contrast yarn K11 sts; replace these sts on the left needle and continue knitting keeping pattern correct. Work rounds 22–38 from chart.

Fourth finger:

Using MC and CC3 alternately, K9 sts, CO5, put 46 sts onto length of contrast yarn, K9; 23 sts.

Working in the round keeping pattern correct, (as for palm) knit until finger measures 5.5cm/2.25in or 0.5cm/0.25in shorter than required length.

Shape tip:

Change to CC1, K1 round.

Next round: (K2tog) 11 times, K1. 11 sts dec; 12 sts rem.

Next round: K.

Next round: (K2tog) 6 times. 6 sts dec; 6 sts rem.

Break yarn, thread through sts, pull tight, fasten off. Take end through to inside.

Extend hand:

Return to sts on length of yarn, re-join MC and CC3, keeping pattern correct, knit all round 46 sts, PUK 5 sts from base of fourth finger; 51 sts total.

Keeping pattern correct K 4 rounds in MC and CC3.

Third finger:

Keeping pattern correct, K7 sts, put 32 sts onto length of contrast yarn, CO4 using MC and CC3 alternately, K12; 23 sts.

Working in the round keeping pattern correct, knit until finger measures 7cm/2.75 in, or 0.5cm/0.25in shorter than required length.
Shape tip as fourth finger.

Second finger:
Keeping pattern correct, K7 sts from contrast yarn, PUK 4 sts from the base of the third finger, K7 sts from contrast yarn, CO 5 sts using MC and CC3 yarn alternately; 23 sts. Working in the round, keeping pattern correct, knit until finger measures 7.5cm/3in, or 0.5cm/0.25in shorter than required length.
Shape tip as fourth finger.

First finger:
Keeping pattern correct, K18 sts from contrast yarn, MC and CC3 yarns alternately PUK 5 sts; 23 sts.
Working in the round keeping pattern correct knit until finger measures 7cm/2.75in, or 0.5cm/0.25in shorter than required length.
Shape tip as fourth finger.

Thumb:
Using MC and CC3 alternately pick up and knit 11 sts (loops) from bottom line of waste yarn, and 14 sts from top row working into ends of opening as necessary; 25 sts.
Working in the round keeping pattern correct knit in speckle pattern until thumb measures 6cm/2.25in or 0.5cm/0.25in shorter than required length.

Shape the tip:
Change to Dark Navy, k 1 round.
Next round: (K2tog) 12 times, K1. 12 sts dec; 13 sts rem.
Next round: K.
Next round: (K2tog) 6 times. 6 sts dec; 7 sts rem.
Break yarn, thread through sts, pull tight, fasten off. Take end through to inside.

Left glove
Knit as right glove to*
Reading chart from right to left, changing colours where indicated, work from Left Glove chart rounds 1–20.
NB rounds 2, 20 and 38 are purled.

Left hand Boreal chart.

Place thumb:

Next round (chart round 21): Keeping pattern correct, K19, using length of contrast yarn K11 sts; replace these sts on the left needle and continue knitting keeping pattern correct.

Work rounds 22–38 from chart.

Knit fingers, hand extension and thumb as right glove.

Finishing:

Darn in all ends, closing any gaps at the base of the fingers as necessary. Give the gloves a light press with a hot iron and damp cloth or according to instructions given with the yarn.

And on to Customization and Designing...

If you have been inspired by gloves in this chapter, the stories of their survival, and of the people who knitted them, and of those who have kept the skills alive, then read on to Chapter 4, for ideas for making gloves that are your own works of art.

GET CREATIVE: DESIGN FOR GLOVE KNITTERS

Design a Pair of Gloves

Through our craft, glove knitters embark on a journey. Typically, the journey starts with making gloves from supplied patterns, as personal replicas of the original. Working from a pattern practises, develops and hones the technical skills and processes needed in knitting gloves. A sense of achievement is felt when the end product looks like the illustration on the screen or the pattern leaflet. That is what many knitters do, whether they are knitting gloves or other items. Many knitters are content to leave it at that. They decide to have a go at, say, a Sanquhar glove, they obtain the pattern and specified yarn, and they follow it to completion.

Some, however, seek more. The glove patterns offered are not quite what they want. They decide, therefore, to adapt these in terms of yarns used, their properties, colour and so on. Such adaptation may cause frustration if the result falls short of what had been intended, but often, with some persistence, a good result is obtained. Some examples are shown later in this chapter.

Without necessarily recognizing it, knitters who adapt and modify have engaged in a process, a process that is called design. Again, many knitters of gloves will stop at this point, having satisfied themselves that they know enough about their craft to experiment. For a few, however, and

hopefully including the readers of this book, and in the same way as for a restless traveller, the journey continues. Where a creative urge combines with technical skills, gloves can be created from their own design inspiration that are original, aesthetically pleasing, and good to wear. For the knitter who produces such gloves (or other garment), this is a significant achievement.

The creative talent that is used in producing gloves from scratch does not, however, reside in some latent genius. Realizing that, talent productively requires different skills and associated tools to complement technical ability. These skills are those of the designer.

The rest of this chapter examines this process of design, from simple adaptations to starting from scratch, as well as introducing the main tools that a textile designer, and glove designer in particular, can use to generate creativity and put it into practice. This chapter is in two sections: the first part looks at adapting and customizing existing designs, covering various approaches to give hesitant designers confidence. The second part looks at the design process, beginning with a design source or inspiration, and working through the making of a moodboard and on to design sheets. An individually crafted pair will be the result of following the moodboard and design sheets with colour and fabric selection, swatching or sampling, and working out the construction of the gloves.

What is 'Designing?'

What does 'design' mean? In this context, design is the process of making choices or selections about how something will be made and how it will look. Many knitters are cautious about design, preferring to knit from patterns in yarn that is specified, as already described. But designing is an enjoyable, creative process allowing the opportunity to play with colours, images, yarns, stitches and ideas. It is an opportunity for self-expression, and a show of creativity and originality.

>   Design is fun!
>   It is a chance to play!
>   A chance to be unique!
>   A chance to express yourself!

I believe that everyone is creative, but that some people have more chance to demonstrate their creativity. Gloves are an ideal canvas on which to have a go at designing, and this can enable and empower you to express your creativity to the maximum!

Given the wonderful selection of yarns and tools that are available now, it seems an ideal time to add individuality to what's being knitted. Gloves are a perfect way to make a start on a one-off design as they take small amounts of yarn and can match or contrast with existing clothes. They also make a great present. New and different stitches can be tried around the cuffs or on the hands. The fit can be tested during knitting and need not be crucial. If this is you, the reader, and you feel ready to dip into designing, please read on! You may discover that you enjoy it and that you have untapped wells of creativity!

Adapting Existing Designs

The first stage in designing and making is often copying. That is what most knitters do when they use a pattern for the instructions for making a garment or other item. It is a good idea to follow a pattern to start with to get the idea of method and construction. When I decided I was going to knit patterned gloves, I used published patterns in the four variations and knitted them all. I then knitted a Mary Allen glove from Sue Leighton-White's pattern. Doing that gave me the skills

Personal Note

I trained as a knitwear and knitted fabric designer as a mature student, and have the zeal of the converted. I made knitwear and many other textiles before I had any design training, but I believe that what I make after this education is of better quality. It is more thought out, more considered, and takes into account many aspects of functionality, appearance and meaning. These qualities may not be apparent in an obvious way but are embedded into what I make because of the design process that I have undertaken both before and during the making.

Throughout this chapter, most of the illustrations and other materials are taken from my own sketchbooks and working notes. They have not been staged or redone, and so they are real life examples, and that way, it is hoped that they are of maximum interest and value. Many are also scruffy and untidy; process is not often neat! They show the work of designing that underpins the production of an original artefact, whether gloves or whatever. It is the final result that counts, not the sketchbooks. Feel free to write shopping lists in the corner of the page! These notes and scribbles were not made for showing: they are part of the process of exploring possibilities and making choices that I am happy to share.

and techniques needed to continue to adaptations and then to my own designs.

Apparently the biggest selling colour of a yarn is often the colour used on the knitting pattern front cover illustration, this being particularly true when patterns were printed paper leaflets. But choosing a different colour for a garment can be a design decision! However, this has started to change as knitting has moved on-line, with sites such as Ravelry and the availability of patterns digitally. Options are now sometimes given for different yarns so that the maker can choose what to knit with. Confident knitters may be used to adapting existing patterns and customizing their knitting with personal touches. Gloves are ideal for trying out these types of changes for those who are less confident. The sections that follow provide some suggestions.

Playing with Colours

Mini skeins are ideal for the fingers of gloves.

Using the pattern for the plain gloves from Chapter 1, try stripes of different colours – use stash and small amounts of leftovers. Mini skeins of yarn would be put to good use here. Each skein in the set shown is a slightly different composition from the others, but this would hardly matter for the few yards needed for a finger or thumb. Add stripes around the cuff or a few rows of colour patterning around the hand between the thumb and the fingers. Remember to keep the knitting loose if it is stranded! Make every finger and the thumbs different colours.

Gloves knitted with a self-striping sock yarn.

Knitting gloves using a self-striping sock yarn gives a good effect and also means that coordinating hands and feet is possible! Sock yarns usually have a blend of wool and polyamide (nylon), which means that whatever is knitted with them will be hard wearing – which is good for gloves as well as socks. (There are yarns that include silk or mohair to give the extra strength, ideal for knitters who wish to avoid the use of oil-derived synthetics.) There are so many different types of self-striping yarns now that will give different effects, depending on the length of the colour changes. Also, the effect will vary between the hand and the fingers due to the difference in the number of stitches. The pair shown is knitted with a yarn with a small amount of contrast colour, orange, in between longer stretches of blue.

Texture

Texture can be introduced to gloves from purl stitches, as in Patterns 2 and 6, to lace, cables, rib, bobbles and twisted stitches. Keep the colours simple and the yarn smooth. There is no point in knitting cables in fluffy or bobbly yarn, nor in yarn that changes colour a lot. Smooth, worsted spun yarns show texture to its best effect. This could vary from a section of rib for the back of the hand to an all-over texture such as the gloves illustrated here, which use a small all-over broken rib pattern. The key to using a textured stitch is to calculate for the fabric to contract because of the texture – more stitches may be needed around the hands and fingers. The same applies to cables, as their structure is usually based on a

Gloves with a small texture pattern.

rib stitch set-up. Also bear in mind that a textured fabric will be warmer as it is slightly thicker than plain smooth fabric, especially when knitted in a wool or wool-mix yarn. The extra thicknesses in the textured fabric will trap tiny pockets of air, which will warm up fast.

Pattern 6 'Vintage Inspiration' is a pattern for textured gloves in a broken rib, like the gloves pictured, but many other small-stitch patterns could be substituted. A textured fabric such as this also gives some extra elasticity and leeway in the fit of the gloves.

Style and Construction

The simple hand warmers illustrated were designed in collaboration with the London menswear designer, John Alexander Skelton, as part of his twelfth collection, in early 2022. They are the simplest form of hand covering, made from a rectangle of fabric seamed up the side leaving an opening for the thumb. These are, in fact, knitted on a knitting machine in a knit 2 purl 2 rib, which gives them a good fit on many sizes of hand. Each is in narrow stripes in two colours of pure wool, giving maximum warmth. They are comfortable and convenient to wear, giving fingers access to screens or to tools if tasks such as writing need to be done. These are more convenient for wearing when doing tasks such as writing than fingerless mitts.

The style of a glove is quite easily changed, in fact the adaptations are often easier to knit than a full glove if fingers are omitted. Particularly if touch screens need to

Mittens adapted from gloves.

be used by the wearer, then a hand covering that allows access to fingers might be more useful than full gloves. Using the pattern for plain gloves from Chapter 1, and adapting according to what is wanted, the amount of yarn available and so on, look back at the illustration that shows all the different types of gloves and hand coverings that are possible in Chapter 1.

Some suggestions:

- Finish the glove just above the knuckles for a fingerless style. Try on the glove for length, knit about four rounds in rib, and cast off in rib. Complete the thumb to the length wanted.
- Knit the fingers and thumb to the length wanted, and cast off each finger separately. To prevent the edge curling, knit a couple of rounds in rib before casting off in rib, unless a curled edge is preferred. This style, known at the time as 'miser mitts', was really fashionable in the 1970s and 1980s.
- Turn the glove into a mitten by continuing to knit the hand, and then shape the top. This can be done in several ways, but a fun way is the spiral shaping from the fingertips of the glove in Chapter 2. Use the same principle to divide the stitches into sets of three, and start to decrease at these points in every round. Decreases can also be worked in sets of four on each round at the edges of the mitten, such as the toe shaping for many socks. Many Scandinavian mitts are decreased right to a point at the top of the hand. However, this is totally optional.

Simple hand warmers.

If a flat top is wanted for a mitten, finish knitting when the hand is the length that is wanted, and join the two sets of stitches from the front and back with grafting, or Kitchener stitch. An alternative is to turn the work inside out and work a three-needle cast-off. Worked on the right side of the work this gives a ridge, which may or may not be wanted. The knitter chooses!

Gloves for using screens may be knitted in three ways:

- To allow access to screens, the tips can be omitted from the thumbs and other fingers as thought necessary.
- Vertical slits can be made in the thumb tip to allow the thumb to poke out. This can be done by knitting backwards and forwards rather than in the round for the top half of the thumb.
- Horizontal slits can be constructed by casting off half the stitches around the thumb or finger and then casting back on over the opening. The knitting is then continued. This is the same process as that used in the construction at the base of the fingers and thumbs.

Size

The size of the object knitted depends on the size of the yarn and the needles used. Size *does* matter when making garments that are fitted or supposed to have any correspondence with the body, and getting it right is often a challenge for the knitter. This is perhaps why garments such as cowls, wraps, shawls, scarves and stoles are so popular for contemporary knitters. When hand knitting was done principally to make garments for the knitter or their family, size was much more critical and the subject of much angst. In fact, the ill-fitting jumper knitted by a well-meaning relative has entered folklore in some parts of the world. While size is not so crucial for the glove knitter, it is still better to aim for gloves that fit their intended wearer.

The most straightforward way to do this is by changing yarn or needle size, perhaps both, using an existing pattern. Any of the patterns in this book, or any other glove pattern, can be made larger or smaller by changing either of these components. The plain glove from Chapter 1, knitted in a thicker yarn with a larger needle size, will fit a bigger hand. Conversely, using a finer yarn will produce a smaller glove. The written instructions for Sanquhar gloves in the 1950s provided by *The People's Friend* magazine were to create smaller or bigger versions by using smaller or bigger needles and yarn. They said that 'Directions are the same for every size', and went on to tell the knitter to use 2-ply wool for children's gloves, 3-ply for women's and 4-ply for men's along with a bigger needle. Because the patterns have to fit around a particular number of stitches it is not possible to alter the size without spoiling the stitch pattern, so the yarn and therefore the size of the knitting itself has to change instead.

Multi-Size Patterns for Gloves

There are many multi-size patterns for gloves available – the following are just a few ideas:

- The on-line knitters and makers website 'Ravelry' is a good source of patterns, many of them free.
- Anne Budd's book *The Knitter's Handy Book of Patterns* includes multi-size and multi-gauge instructions for gloves and mittens (*see* Bibliography).
- Vintage knitting pamphlets and leaflets such as *Woolcraft* have instructions for basic gloves for men, women and children. These are available on-line for members, from the Knitting & Crochet Guild (*see* Resources).

Substituting Yarn and Organizing Yarn

Gloves are a good project for small amounts of yarn – for instance hand-spun yarn, hand-dyed yarn, or very expensive yarns such as cashmere or even qiviut, as discussed in Chapter 1. Because they take a relatively small amount, the yarn for a pair of gloves will not be exorbitantly expensive. If using a single skein or ball of yarn it's a good idea to divide it into two before starting to knit, so that progress can be judged, and design decisions made accordingly. In that way, the yarn will last to the same point in both gloves.

Another way of making yarn go further is to reverse the colours on one glove so that the main colour for one hand becomes the contrast colour for the other. An example of this is the pair knitted for a friend, using two colours of vintage 3-ply pure wool.

Left and right hands with opposite main colour yarn.

What's in the Stash?

Gloves are a good way of using up stash yarns, and it's great to have a go at gloves without having to worry about the price of some especially precious skein of yarn! They don't use up a huge amount, not like, say, a blanket or throw, but a pair will use a skein or ball that would not be enough for a larger project. Check the weight and length of the yarn that will be used, and if necessary, make adjustments. For instance, the plain gloves in Chapter 1 use just a little more than 50g of yarn. If planning to use a ball or skein that weighs that amount, work fewer rounds of rib in the cuff, or add a few stripes of another yarn. Be prepared to have some contrasting fingers!

Gloves for friends using up stash.

The red and green pairs of gloves pictured here are knitted from the Dales pattern with some customization. Different shades of the same colour are used, and this gives a lively effect and a workable solution to using up yarns, as shown in these pairs, knitted for friends. Both pairs had to have fingers completed in yarns that are not an exact match because the original yarn ran out. The yarns used were from my large stash of vintage 3-ply wools, and I asked my friends what colours they liked the best. They chose colours that I didn't have a lot of – it might have been better to have offered a more limited choice of colours based on how much there was of each!

Having explored ways of adapting, customizing and generally altering gloves from existing patterns, let's now have a look at the process of customizing a pair.

Customizing

The Personal Touch Applied to Traditional Patterns

Some of the earliest knitted gloves still extant have either name, dates or initials knitted in, as is the case in the Yorkshire Dales and Sanquhar in Scotland, described in Chapter 3. A pair of wool gloves, location now unknown, had the date '1818' and the owner's initials knitted into the palm. Initials and dates have been used traditionally around the wrist of gloves to customize them, like those belonging to Marianne Clarke and Lord Howe shown in Chapter 2. This is also seen in those from the Yorkshire Dales and Sanquhar from the nineteenth century, and was probably not only a way of identifying the gloves' owner, but a mark of status and an indication of how special the patterned knitted glove was. Perhaps there was a social cachet in commissioning a personalized pair to own or to give away?

The pattern for the Dales glove in Chapter 3 lends itself to this treatment, and those gloves and Sanquhar gloves traditionally have the owner's initials worked in them. The customization does not have to be literally the date made; it could be the owner's date of birth or another significant year. The style of the letters and/or numbers that is chosen will depend on personal choice, but at its simplest is either 'old fashioned', like those on the M.E.A. gloves in Chapter 3, or 'modern' as on those pictured.

An alphabet and numbers in a 'Dales' style are given in Appendix II at the end of the book.

Or how about changing the motifs inside the grid of Sanquhar gloves? In fact, there are several modern versions of the Sanquhar glove, including a Christmas theme and another with little skulls. Shown is a pair knitted for a son with a mathematical bent, where the patterns inside the grid of the Sanquhar Duke pattern have been replaced with

A modern style for the initials and date.

The Sanquhar pattern with a modern twist: first order logic symbols. (Courtesy Michele Poulin-Alfeld)

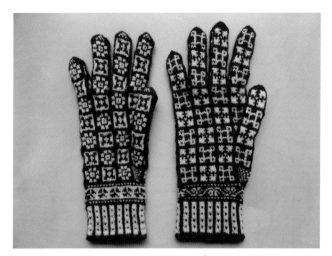

Sanquhar-style gloves with customized symbols, designed and knitted by Nancy Bush. (Courtesy Nancy Bush)

symbols from the system for writing first order logic. Using the Sanquhar grid as a starting point, the squares can be filled with many different motifs, as these next two pairs show.

Nancy Bush, an expert on Estonian knitting, designed and knitted the red and blue pair pictured for Estonian friends in 2015. She says:

I knit them from traditional Sanquhar instructions but changed the patterns to be more 'Estonian'. The red ones have a cross in one square, and as close as I could get to the symbol used to designate a site of cultural or historic interest in the other. I gave this pair to a friend who works at the Estonian Open Air Museum, it seemed fitting. The blue ones have patterns I found on Estonian embroidery or knitting. I added black in the cuff to use the colors (sic) of the Estonian flag in them. They went to a friend who is a former Estonian Olympic track star.

In a further twist on the Sanquhar pattern, British knitter Sue Carne designed and knitted the Quick Response (QR) code into the back of the hands on the black and white gloves pictured. They were exhibited at a science fair in Manchester, northern England, long before the QR code had become as common as it is today. Sue has explored Sanquhar and Dales gloves as well as some from Kashmir (*see* the Resources section at the back of the book for the link to her on-line space where some of these can be seen and enjoyed).

sanQR = Sanquhar + QR code gloves. (Courtesy Sue Carne)

Bespoke Gloves

Any knitwear can be customized with particular motifs, and gloves lend themselves to this. The pair illustrated was designed in collaboration with the prospective owner, a proficient flute player and musician. The design was based on the pattern and construction of the traditional 3-ply wool gloves from the Dales and Sanquhar, which have about eighty stitches around the cuff. The vintage Sanquhar colours, old gold and chocolate brown, were chosen after seeing a vintage pair in an exhibition. Fortunately there was wool in these colours in my stash, so these went on to the sketchbook page along with an image (photocopy!) of the vintage gloves.

An outline of the musician's hand was an essential next step, which then became heavily annotated during the designing and knitting process. He lives in Yorkshire, so an easy choice for the pattern on the back of the hands was a Yorkshire one. Of the three, the tree of life was selected.

Sketchbook page.

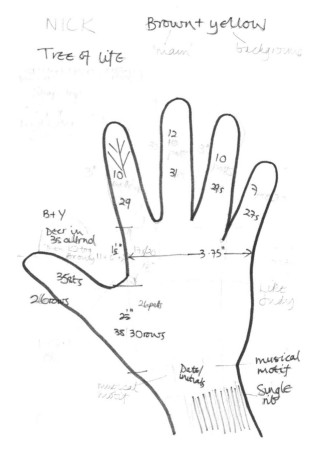

Outline of hand.

The cuffs being knitted.

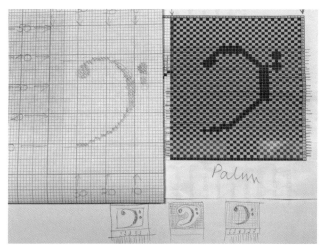

Designing the bass clef.

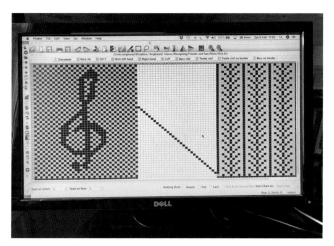

Treble clef on screen.

Trying on.

Gloves for a musician, backs.

Gloves for a musician, palms.

Initials went on the left hand, and the year of making went round the right wrist above the 'Dale's style' two-colour, knit-one, purl-one rib. The wrists have a line of musical notes round the cuffs, and a treble and a bass clef on the palms of the hands.

These ideas and decisions can be traced through the notes and diagrams that were made during the designing and knitting process, which were not made with an audience in mind! What starts as a tentative pencil outline ends up as a chart using knitting design software on the laptop. After some calculations, knitting was started. Because there are some long spaces between the colours the brown wool was caught in at the back of the yellow, during the knitting, often known rather misleadingly as 'weaving'. This gives the fabric some texture, but means that long strands of yarn are kept close to the fabric and won't be caught when putting the gloves on and taking them off. It's a matter of opinion whether you think this is messy or if you think it gives the fabric some life.

How did I work out the treble and bass clefs? Firstly, they were drawn on squared paper freehand (*see* page 101). A chart was made for both gloves, the right with the treble clef on the palm, and the left with the bass clef on the palm. This was done using Intwined Studio, a knitting design software package, no longer supported, for the back and front of both hands. The large gap in between them indicates the thumb construction, which was asymmetric, the line of squares indicating the increases on every row on one side of the thumb gusset. The prospective owner tried them on with only the thumbs to be knitted. The tree of life pattern continues up the fingers, which is not usually the case with Dales gloves. The completed gloves are shown in the last two images.

So, a design that started out in the colours of a vintage Sanquhar glove, changed bit by bit into something of a Dales glove – that is, the rib, initials, date and tree of life patterns, then a different thumb construction, and finally allied with some freestyle motifs on the palms and wrists for the musical additions. So truly a one-off pair!

Having had some fun modifying, then adding individuality and special features, let's now look at designing 'from scratch'.

The Design Process: An Overview

Even for an item as small as a pair of gloves, or perhaps *especially* for an item as small as a pair of gloves, the design process is worth following and will give the product a refine-ment reflecting the thought processes that have gone into it. In creative design courses and for many professional design-ers, the starting point is a *moodboard*. There need not be anything elaborate about it, in fact it can be as simple as a postcard and some yarn wraps, or it can be an assemblage of images, fabrics, found objects and so on, as described later. A moodboard is a constant reference for the designer in any context, with or without a formal design background. This can also be thought of as the *design brief* if it is expressed in words rather than images.

From that, by selecting colours, ideas for patterns, shapes and other details, *design sheets* can be made. These might consist of any kind of visualizations of the design ideas: drawings, sketches, electronic images, collages and photocopies. Now is probably the time to start to knit – just a *swatch* at this stage – the part that most people seem to hate!

From the ideas on the design sheet and the swatch, a *final design* is selected. Using the information from the swatch about tension/gauge, calculate the number of stitches to cast on.

- Start to knit
- Review at frequent intervals
- Try on
- Undo
- Repeat!
- Compare the outcome with the design ideas – how do they match?

So now we'll look at each of these stages in turn.

Designing from a Design Inspiration

What is Design Inspiration?

Moving on from making by following instructions and adapting existing designs, let's start from scratch with the design inspiration. Textile designers take all sorts of things as inspiration. A shortlist might include animals, buildings, cars, doors …. all the way to zebras! If you are designing and making for someone in particular, it gives more meaning if there's a link between your inspiration and that person, as in the example we've already looked at, of the musician. The result can make a special present.

Some Real Examples of Design Sources

These are some of my design inspirations for gloves:

- Wildflowers in Pembrokeshire
- Pebbles and stones on an Anglesey beach
- Twigs and gorse bushes in December
- Black and white tweed fabric woven in Wales
- Snow and grass on a path in the Pennines
- Deserted wooden farm buildings painted white

These are more often than not photos taken on my phone. They usually get printed out and put in the sketchbook, forming the basis for adding ideas in coloured pencil and possible yarns. Buildings and structures such as fences are good for knitwear design ideas too, as they have strong geometric elements, but I have used other textiles including Welsh quilts and patchworks.

In fact, there is barely anything that cannot be used as a design inspiration!

Moodboards

A standard way of beginning to design is by making a moodboard, which is a collection of visuals of all types. These are a useful tool for all types of visual activity, such as decorating a room or planning a stage set, so it's as good a place to start as any.

Your moodboard could be a single postcard and some lengths of yarn, or a compilation of various materials, suggested below. It could in fact be a page in a scrapbook, or pinned up on a noticeboard. Words can also be added to prompt or reinforce ideas. The most important point is that the moodboard means something to *you*, the creative knitter. It doesn't have to make sense to anyone else, and it doesn't have to be a work of art.

Moodboards can be 'in real life' – that is, actually made of cardboard, photographs, shells and so on, but they can also be digital. Both sorts will be discussed now.

Making a Moodboard 'In Real Life'

What should go on a moodboard? How big should it be? Can it be in a sketchbook, or should it be free standing? The answer to all these questions is – it depends! And it's your choice. And you don't have to have one at all, but it's more fun if you do! Shown here are the tools that might be

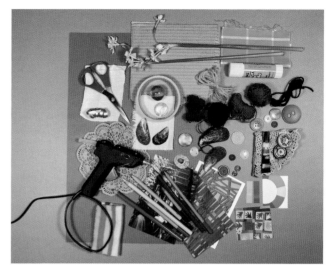

Tools and materials for a moodboard. (With thanks to Brynmor Watson)

needed, along with many ideas for what *could* go on a moodboard. Let's start by looking at an 'in real life' moodboard.

The Background for a Moodboard

The background can be any size from, say, A4 upwards. It does not have to be an expensive sheet of pristine mountboard, although it could be just that if that's what you want! Cut-up cardboard boxes are fine, backs of posters, calendars, whatever is to hand. Reduce, reuse and recycle as much as possible!

Tools for a Moodboard

You will need various glues. A glue gun is handy, as is spray glue, but there is no need to spend money on either of these. Stick glue bought in any supermarket is fine. Masking tape is useful, as are magic tape and double-sided tape.

Make the moodboard with whatever is to hand, and don't feel that money has to be spent, certainly not in large quantities. A stapler fixes yarns and paper in a way that doesn't come apart after a short while, which glue can be prone to do.

Cutting implements such as scissors and/or pinking shears for fabrics need to be at hand, but remember that ripped edges can give more life than immaculately cut edges. This is true for paper as well as fabrics. But if the mood is crisp and clean, then of course have crisp edges!

Look at the example moodboard pictured for some further ideas, and compare what is to hand with the list in the box.

Collecting Items to go on a Moodboard

Coloured papers – scraps will do
Wrapping paper – again, scraps are fine
Magazine pages – tear out favourite pieces
Postcards, old and new
Sweet wrappers
Pressed flowers and leaves: twigs, grasses, petals
Buttons and beads
Yarns/threads/ribbons
Fabric scraps and swatches
Shells, marbles, stones
Bits of pottery
Broken jewellery and trinkets

Have a shoebox or crate handy to drop things into so there's a good selection to work with when the time comes.

Laying Out the Moodboard

Begin by laying things out, perhaps starting with a key image. Add to this, each time asking if what you have added 'fits' or says the right things about your story. The moodboard can be pinned up on a noticeboard or straight on to a wall, or it can be glued to a backing. It can be large, if space permits, or it could be as small as A4.

Everything can be done quite fast – if there's space, pin it up so that it can be looked at from a distance. Come back to it after a time interval – say, overnight – to see if it's still 'saying' what you want it to.

When everything's selected, get it glued down!

Real Examples of Moodboards

These pages, completely different from each other, illustrate my thought processes and selection of visuals at the start of a project. Both are taken from my sketchbooks, which are A3 landscape in size.

The moodboard on a theme of the Faroe Islands was the start of the design process for two pairs of gloves for friends who have spent time in the Faroe Islands. These are images of Faroese motifs, and a couple of photos of an actual piece of knitwear from the Knitting & Crochet Guild collection. Other images came from visitors to Faroe. This was the jumping-off point for the patterning on the gloves. It is very much an 'everyday' type of moodboard: nothing three dimensional, but still exploring ideas of pattern and identifying what

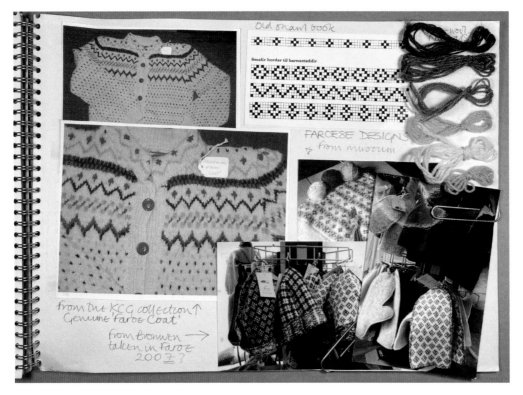

Moodboard on a theme of the Faroe Islands.

Exploring a bright colour palette.

distinguishes Faroese knitting. The yarn wraps are neutral and natural colours, the sort that might be associated with undyed Faroe sheep, although the genuine Faroe garment has pink or faded red in it.

In a speculative frame of mind, the bright colour palette page was put together from a range of materials: there is some printing here from a sketchbook from about thirty years ago, and photographs and screen shots and scans from other sources. One of the fabrics is a vintage skirt from the early 1970s! The yarns are all stash vintage 3-ply.

It can be seen that each of these pages would take the designer in a different direction: the first into natural colours with small geometric designs adapted from those in the images, and the second into bright colours, with stripes or checks and possibly with different glove forms as suggested by the long gloves in the image on the right-hand side of the page. The result of following one or the other will be very different, and that is the designer's choice.

Digital Moodboards

Moodboards can also be made on screen, on phones (perhaps a little small?), tablets or laptops. Here there is less chance to 'play', but they can be a useful resource, especially for those short of space for spreading out with boards and glue. Using images collected for the purpose in a folder can be a good start. With cameras on phones and tablets there is no excuse for missing possible design sources; however, the downside is that choosing from so many images can be difficult. Try to edit soon after taking pictures.

Resources for Digital or On-line Moodboards

Pinterest is perhaps the most commonly used digital storage place for images and ideas. Some designers use on-line sites such as Pinterest to construct moodboards, and these can be useful as electronic storage places for images. It can also be a useful place to keep design ideas, which could include your own photos, images or scans, as well as any that you find on-line. A search of terms such as 'textile moodboards' brings up many versions of these that can be browsed.

There are websites that enable a moodboard to be made, and which even give step-by-step instructions, such as Canva.com (*see* Resources section at the back of this book).

A Visual Resource: The Lookbooks of Brooklyn Tweed

Lookbook from Brooklyn Tweed.

Brooklyn Tweed, the American yarn and knitwear design company, has a strong emphasis on design, and issues 'lookbooks' for each of their collections. Lookbooks are a set of highly selected and edited images that convey the type of look and garments in a range. The lookbook sets the tone and ideas for each collection, and presents all the designs in that collection together. The lookbooks can be found via their website, and the title page for the *Holiday 21* collection is illustrated, this being just one example. The smallest details are crucial here, from the setting in the forest, the suggestion of hiking and being outside in the forest, and the glimpse of the rolled-up picnic blanket and the tin coffee pot, all set for a cosy time with lots of nice warm woollens.

Words can add a lot to a mood. Here under the image they say '...Breathe in the crisp air and linger a moment by the campfire, cozy (sic) in your new sweater...' Do go and browse their other lookbooks at the link in the Resources section at the back of this book, as it is a rich seam of high quality visuals.

The Design Brief

At this stage it is useful for some people to think about what's going to be made in words as well as images. A design brief just sets down what is to be done, and can be useful to define some clear limits. It's easy to become overwhelmed with the amount of choice. The brief could just identify the main features of what is going to be made, as described here:

- Full finger gloves – mittens – simple handwarmers?
- Yarn – stash – bought for the purpose? How much – what sort – fibre – thickness?
- Cost – expensive or not? Does it matter?
- Colour – what is wanted – particular colours – to match or contrast – to express an allegiance – a personal preference – or just what is there?
- Construction – simple – peasant thumb – other types – full fingers – shaping?
- Patterning – all over – some plain – complicated – simple?
- Time available – is there plenty of time to do this? Is there a deadline – a birthday or Christmas? Are they going to be a present? What sort of time is available?

If all these questions are answered, then along with the visual starting point of the moodboard, the designing is really under way. Of course, the two things work in tandem, because if the moodboard is all light colours and gauzy fabrics, then the brief would probably specify a light cotton or linen yarn and an open-work glove. And vice versa, of course.

A Real Example of a Design Brief from 2020

- **What is wanted?** Hand-knitted gloves for a present for a special birthday.
- **What yarn?** This has to be silk, as the person can't wear wool due to eczema on their hands. Silk also has the connotation and price of being exclusive. It is also practical, as it is warm and hard-wearing.
- **What colours?** The person has been a lifelong supporter of Leeds Rugby League team, the Rhinos, so their colours are an obvious choice – royal blue and a golden yellow. Fortunately these colours are available in the silk yarn that is most suitable.
- **What pattern?** For a Yorkshire born and bred man, it has to be a Yorkshire Dales pattern – which one?
- **Time-scale:** The birthday was a real deadline, so the designing and knitting of these gloves had to be a priority.
- **Cost?** The gloves were a present, so the cost does not have to be calculated in monetary terms.

From Moodboard to Design Sheets

From the moodboard, start making colour choices. If stash yarns are being used or if yarns are already available, these can be added to the moodboard. Using the design inspiration, the yarns can be chosen and grouped using small amounts to test different combinations.

Design Sheets

From the moodboard, move towards a design sheet: what is it? Just what it sounds like: ideas for designs all in one place. The yarns might be added at moodboard stage, or they can appear again on the design sheet, possibly after more selection has been done.

The point of design sheets, or pages in a sketchbook, is that they allow you, the designer, an opportunity to think through all the possibilities before you start making.

Here all the possible yarns can be collected together. Ideas about shape, size and style can be gathered, as well as colours. Collect the yarns together and place little lengths of them to put on the design sheet. They can be made into bows, or small skeins, or wrapped around a card, whichever is more appropriate. Or they can just be stapled on – whatever works.

Real Examples of a Design Sheet
The first design-sheet sketchbook page explores just a few of the quilts of Gee's Bend (those made in a remote village in the southern USA, and now well known from exhibitions and publications), looking at the colours used and exploring them to try to identify what it is that makes them so appealing. Then the colours can be explored by finding matches for them in knitting yarns, and in this case coloured pencils. Large sets of art materials are not necessary for any of these processes. An A4 sketchbook from the supermarket and a set of a dozen coloured pencils is more than enough.

This second page explores some of the possibilities suggested by the design inspiration using the yarns available. It is a lot quicker to draw several variations and use coloured pencils rather than setting out to knit the variations. Mock-ups can be made at this stage with coloured papers or using digital software if those methods are preferred. Photocopied gloves can be drawn on or coloured in to explore ideas about

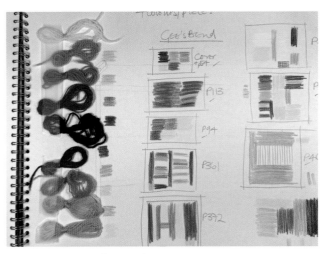

A design sheet – colour and yarns.

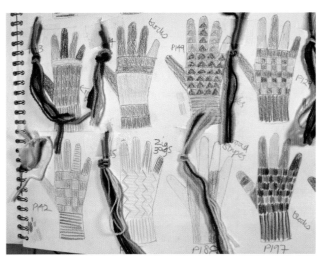

Design sheet for multicoloured gloves.

patterns. I have even drawn on a pair of rubber gloves to test out where the patterns will lie!

Using Templates

A hand-shaped template can save a lot of time, especially for those who are not confident about drawing. One can be made simply by drawing round a hand, or a search on-line gives plenty in a variety of shapes and positions. With a page of a sketchbook and a template, outlines of several gloves can be drawn, and many variations filled in with coloured pencils or paints, or notes made about design, colour and stitch.

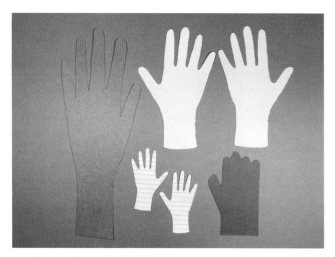

Hand templates.

From Drawing and Thinking to Sampling and Swatching

Now, think about how to start the glove/s: what cast-on might you use? What kind of cuff might be best? Rib? If so, single rib, or 2 knit, 1 purl, two-coloured, perhaps with an extra stitch to break it up? … And so on. All these variations can be sketched out in minutes before making a decision. In fact, sometimes just writing down the possibilities is enough!

Having come quite a long way down the design path in terms of exploring ideas for what is going to be knitted, choosing colours, yarns and stitch constructions, the action now turns to testing these ideas in the form of knitting samples and swatches.

At some point, coming after the moodboard and design sheet stages, it is time to move from the page to the needles. Samples and then swatches need to be made, especially if this is a type of yarn that you have not used before. There is a variety of examples in the image. Some were knitted to test yarn and colour combinations, while others were made to try out stitch patterns. Most of them were testing the type of cast-on to use, while several were knitted to check the relationship between the yarn and the needle size. At least six of them were used as the swatch for subsequent stitch calculations.

Samples for Colour Combinations

Coloured pencils and yarn wraps at design sheet stage will suggest good colour combinations, but there is no substitute

A selection of samples and swatches.

for actually knitting those colours together. To really test your design ideas, this part of the process is *essential*. Sampling intended yarns and patterns in the form of a swatch means that time-wasting mistakes are less likely to be made. Why cast on nearly a hundred stitches in an unknown colour combination that turns out to look awful, when a handful would have done the job?

Sampling will enable the knitter/designer to consider the type of yarn chosen, the patterns that are going to be used, and the colours selected.

The sample knitting is the time to choose, and vary, colours, needle size, stitches, patterns and structure. All these variants, taken together, will make for a sample that is what is wanted – or not! Keep your samples. Attach them to your design sheets or pin them up on a noticeboard. Try not to undo them unless this is absolutely essential. They are a valuable resource and reference.

What is the Difference between a Swatch and a Sample?
Maybe there isn't much difference between a swatch and a sample, but perhaps the best way of thinking about them is like this: a sample is a small piece of knitted fabric that gives an idea of how the intended glove (or other item) may look. Samples can include knitting a yarn on different sizes of needle, trying out various stitch patterns, making

stripes of different widths, and generally just exploring with the ideas that have come from the moodboard and the design sheet.

A swatch is the final piece knitted using the combination of yarn, needle size, colour and stitch construction that has been chosen for the final piece from the samples.

A Real Example of a Swatch
For this swatch the colours were selected from stash yarns as being representative of the stony neutral colours found on a stretch of Anglesey beach captured in a phone picture. Once knitted, even in a small swatch of twenty-four stitches, it confirmed that the colour choice was satisfactory and that knitting could go ahead. The sample was cast on with a Dales-type two-colour method, so that did not need to be resampled.

Swatching for Tension or Gauge

A swatch can then be knitted. If the knitting is in the round, which it will be for gloves, then the sample needs to be knitted this way too. Swatches can be any size from a couple of dozen stitches upwards – whatever is easy to handle and big enough to give a piece of knitting that can indicate the

A swatch and the image that inspired it.

required number of stitches per centimetre or inch. A variety of swatches and some samples are shown in the illustration using different yarns and different numbers of stitches. All are, however, knitted in the round.

If different size needles are used in a swatch, care is needed to mark the change from one size to another. This can be done with marker threads or swing tags.

A Real Example of Designing a Cuff Edge and Hem

These are all sample pieces, of differing sizes, for the cuff edge of a pair of gloves inspired by vintage Estonian gloves. The needle size was varied during this process. A picot hem was tried for some of them, along with some rounds of garter stitch and various two-colour cast-ons. About twelve were worked, not all shown here, before a satisfactory one was selected. This process created a considerable delay to the start of the knitting! The number of stitches was calculated from the sample or swatch that was eventually chosen.

Practical Considerations – Intended Use, Owner

The choice of yarns is key to all that follows in the design and making process – colour, handle, durability, tension/gauge and pattern. Chapter 1 discussed a broad range of yarns and their suitability for gloves, but now precise selections have to be made. The reasons for choosing a pure silk yarn in one case were explained in the section 'Real Example of a Design Brief' given earlier: similar reasons will apply for all choices.

At this stage, practicalities might have to take precedence over purely aesthetic design considerations; for example, if yarn is not available in specific colours in a particular range, then substitutes may have to be made. Obviously this is not ideal, but designing is often about reconciling differing requirements – for instance, wearability versus colour, or touch (handle) versus price. Colours may be especially constrained if vintage yarns are sourced. Slightly different yarns knitted together in colour patterns can give a knitted fabric a life that

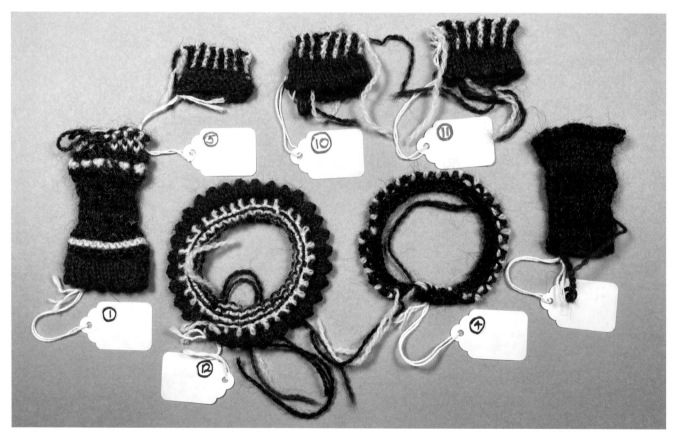

Testing different cast-ons before starting to knit.

can be lacking in completely uniform yarns. Make the most of the difference!

Working Out Size and Construction

Working Out Stitches and Rows

This is where the swatch comes in. It has to be measured across a known number of stitches, and the required number of stitches per centimetre or inch can then be calculated. The same can be done with the rows, but these are not usually so crucial as length, and can often be measured as the knitting proceeds.

As most knitting, especially in wool, has a good degree of stretch, there is some leeway on the sizing. Two things need to be known: tension/gauge and size of the hand. Both need to be measured.

Tension or Gauge
The number of stitches per centimetre or inch is the important information. If the yarn needs it, wash, press, steam or otherwise treat it as instructed on the ball band. Let it cool and settle. Depending on the yarn, especially for pure wools,

A swatch with pins measuring tension/gauge.

it is good to leave it overnight. Measure the swatch lying flat to see what number of stitches there are per centimetre or inch (personal choice of units here) using pins to measure say, 4cm, and then count the number of stitches between the pins.

The Size of the Hand
Measure the width and length of the hand/s you are knitting for – *see* diagram. If the hands are available, then measurements and fittings can be made as the knitting is done. If not, then either an outline of the hand or some measurements are needed. If the gloves are to be a surprise, then standard measurements can be taken from charts and tables on-line.

What Size Should the Glove Be?
If the glove is for a particular person and is not a surprise, then draw round the person's hand. That outline can be used as a template for calculating the number of stitches needed. The work in progress can be held against the outline to check things such as the position of the thumb. This method works well if the knitter and the person being knitted for can liaise for fittings. A 'real life' example of a hand outline was shown in the 'musical' gloves earlier this chapter. If it is a surprise, then informed guesswork is an option!

Working Out Stitches from Measurements

Take the measurements from the diagram for one hand. Unless the hands are significantly different in shape or size, this will be adequate. Help will be needed with the measuring tape!

Use these measurements along with the stitches per centimetre/inch to calculate the number of stitches needed throughout.

Back to the Swatch
The number of stitches multiplied by the hand circumference measurement (a) on the diagram gives the number to cast on. The exact measurement around the hand can be used for this calculation, as it is not usual to have any ease in the fit of a glove. Be prepared to adjust, however, after knitting a

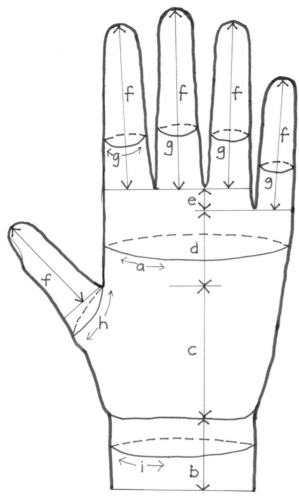

Measurements for custom-fit gloves.

a   circumfrence of palm taken at widest point
b   length of desired cuff
c   length between thumb division and wrist (i.e. crease at base of palm)
d   length between little finger division and thumb division
e   measurement of step between little finger division and base of third finger
f   finger and thumb lengths
g   circumfrence of fingers taken at bottom knuckle
h   circumfrence of thumb taken at bottom knuckle
i   circumfrence of wrist

few rounds, to check that the size looks correct. The best way to do this is to slip the stitches on to a strong thread using a suitable sized wool needle, and try on the glove. With two circular needles it is possible to check the fit while the stitches are on the needles.

Construction

A glove is usually knitted from the wrist upwards, in a series of distinct stages. It is simplest to take these one at a time: the sequence is given here. (It might be useful to look back at the process pictures for knitting the plain glove in Chapter 1 as well as the diagram showing the anatomy of the glove.)

The Stages in Knitting a Glove

1. Cuff or wrist.
2. From the wrist to the fork of the thumb – this includes the thumb gusset.
   Note: The thumb can be knitted as soon as the thumb gusset is complete; this sequence is used in Pattern 6: 'Vintage Inspiration'. It means that the glove can be tried on for size and fit accurately before continuing up the hand.
3. From the fork of the thumb to the base of the fourth finger.
4. Fourth finger – knit.
5. Extend the hand.
6. Knit the fingers – third, second, first.
7. Knit the thumb.
8. Complete by darning in all the ends, and closing any holes in the work.
9. Press, block, wash or finish as wanted!

Let's take each of these in turn.

The Cuff or Wrist

This is measurement (b) on the diagram. Using the figures from the calculations above, cast on and knit the cuff as wanted; remember it does not have to be rib. Chapter 3 examined Estonian gloves with many options for the cuff. Also bear in mind that the cuff does not have to be snug fitting – it could be flared. The pattern for the silk glove in Chapter 2 has a straight cuff with a very small amount of shaping.

If the cuff is ribbed it may be worked on needles a couple of sizes smaller than those used for the main part of the hand. This is not essential however, and vintage patterns tend to use the same size needle for rib and hand. Perhaps this was because people would not have owned many pairs of needles then?

The wrist above the cuff may have a customization, a date or initials: look back to the Dales gloves to see this in action, as well as some of the illustrations.

From the Wrist to the Fork of the Thumb including the Thumb Gusset

This is measurement (c) on the diagram. Look through the patterns in the book to see how the thumb is shaped. The plain glove has a symmetrical gusset with regular increases on each side, as does the Sanquhar-style glove. The silk glove in Chapter 2 has an asymmetrical thumb, which is an interesting and easy one to work because the shaping is worked on every round in the same place. Pattern 5 makes use of the simplest thumb construction, the peasant thumb. All are possible. Use the measurements to work out how many stitches need to be increased in what number of rows to give the shaping.

Calculating the Thumb Gusset Increases

A shaped thumb has to be calculated working out how many stitches should be in the thumb as against how many rows high the thumb should be. It can be useful to have a diagram here to get a sense of how many stitches need to be increased.

The number of stitches to be increased is the number that is needed to go round the thumb divided into the number of rows between the wrist and the fork of the thumb, (e) on the diagram.

Now, the number of stitches to increase above the thumb gusset has to be decided. This can vary from none or one, to several, depending on whether the hand needs to be wider at this stage. It is a matter of judgement.

When to Knit the Thumb

The thumb can be knitted after the thumb gusset is completed, a sequence that is used in Pattern 6: 'Vintage Inspiration'. It means that the glove can be tried on for size and fit accurately before continuing up the hand.

This can also be done with the peasant thumb construction to make trying on a more accurate process.

Choice of Thumb

The simplest construction uses the peasant thumb, as the number of stitches is the same all the way up the hand.

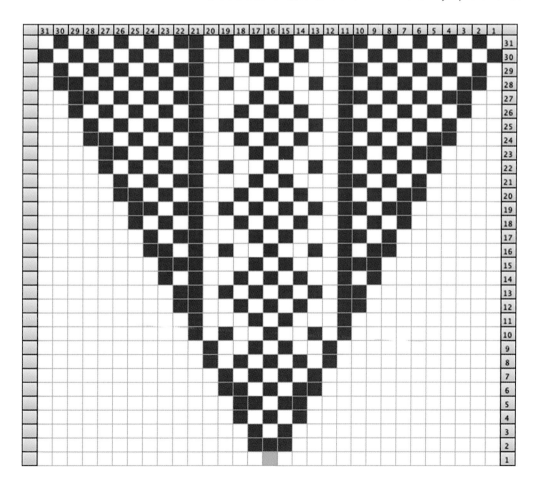

The chart for a patterned thumb.

The thumb is made by knitting a length of scrap thread and then picking up the stitches from it. The thumb in Pattern 5 is made this way.

Check back to Chapter 1 for a detailed description and images of different thumb constructions.

The Hand between the Thumb Division and the Fourth Finger Division

This is measurement (d) on the diagram. From the fork of the thumb to the base of the fourth finger is a good place for some patterning. If it's a stitch pattern that might pull in, then increase around the hand where the pattern starts, and decrease at the end before the fingers start. It is most straightforward to do these increases and decreases on plain rows.

The Fingers

The measurements (f) for length and (g) for circumference are given on the diagram. The patterns in this book have the fourth finger starting a little lower than the others, except for Pattern 3: 'Inspired by Mary Allen' and Pattern 4: 'Inspired by Alba'. If this is a complication too far, then start all the fingers from the same round. Modern patterns tend to allow for this small adjustment to improve the fit of gloves; most vintage patterns do not bother with it. It's a matter of choice and judgement.

Fourth finger – knit: Take a quarter of the stitches on the back and front of the hands. Work out what the stitch count round the fourth finger should be by multiplying the measurement by the stitches per centimetre/inch. Make up any difference by casting on that number of stitches between the front and the back of the hands.

Extend the Hand

This is measurement (e) on the diagram. On the remaining hand stitches, knit a small number of rounds to allow for the lower starting point of the fourth finger. This is not necessary for all hands, and not an essential step for many gloves, such as Pattern 4: 'Inspired by Alba' and Pattern 6: 'Vintage Inspiration'.

Knit the Fingers – Third, Second, First

The measurements (f) and (g) on the diagram are (f) for length and (g) for circumference. If a glove is patterned, then this might determine the patterning on the finger. If the fingers are to be patterned it is best to think about it well before they are started so that the numbers of stitches do not have to be adjusted at their base. However, this can be done in the cast-ons or the pick-up and knits if necessary.

To work out the number of stitches for each finger, take a quarter of the stitches in the back and front of the hand, and add anything from two to three to four to five for the extra width that is needed at the base of the finger. The number of stitches needed around each finger is worked out from the stitches per centimetre/inch and the measurement around the finger.

The length of the fingers can be worked out from the information about the size of the hand required, and the row count of the swatch, whether this is from a diagram, or a set of measurements or actually trying on.

Remember to allow for the shaping of the fingertip when deciding the length, as this will add anything from 0.5 to 1cm or more, so has to be taken into account.

Knit the Thumb

The measurements (f) for length and (h) for circumference are on the diagram. Return to the thumb gusset stitches and knit the thumb to the required length.

Final Note

Calculating the stitches for knitted gloves is not an exact science, although once written down it appears to be. Like many processes, when described in words, this appears to be more laborious and time-consuming than when being done in practice.

There is a certain give and take in all of this, but the final result of all this effort should give a unique, well-fitting glove – an end product that is worth the effort.

Lastly, darn in the ends, close any holes at the base of the fingers, steam, press, wash or block as wanted! Result – a custom-fitting pair of gloves!

Using Knitting Software

As with moodboards, working out the detail of the knitting can be done physically using pencil and paper, or it can be done using knitting software on a device, whether this is your laptop or tablet.

There are programs for charting knitting digitally. Some of these are free to use and some have to be bought. Squared paper is fine for planning out patterns, but after some initial freehand diagrams and rough sketches, a computer program can be much faster. In particular, for generating all-over patterns, and for working out patterns such as dates and initials, the computer can be the glove knitter's friend.

It really is not possible to recommend a specific program as they differ in capability, price, availability and so on – thus it is very much an individual's preference. Some knitters use a spreadsheet as a charting tool.

There are also apps such as Knit Companion that enable the knitter to keep track of their work (*see* the Resources section at the back of the book).

Designing Other Knitwear

All the information and illustrations about designing for gloves can apply to the design of any knitwear, from hats and scarves to garments of any type. Starting with design inspiration, making a moodboard, and drawing design ideas can be done for any garment following the same guidelines. Making a swatch, taking measurements, calculating stitches and rows followed by trying on – the process is the same for any knitted garment. Using moodboards and design sheets can be done for many situations where design decisions have to be made, whether textile related or not!

Designing gloves is a great place to start experimenting with one's own patterns, and also a good opportunity to try different stitches and colour combinations. It should also be fun and enjoyable!

So, if you've got this far, to take it further and to feed your creative imagination, Chapter 5 looks at where gloves can be seen in collections, both 'in real life' and on-line.

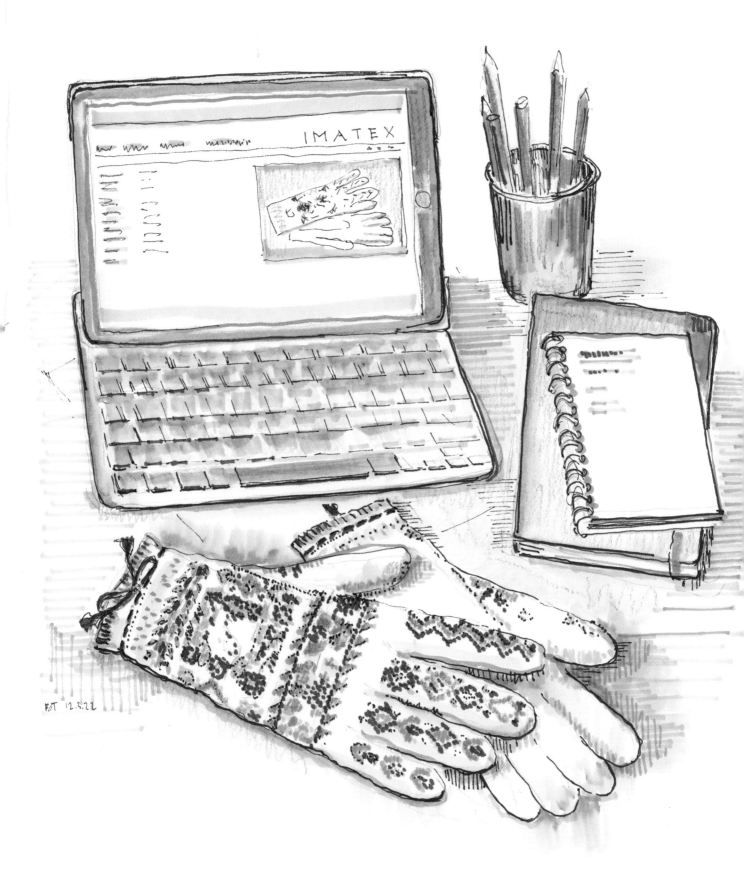

CHAPTER 5

KNITTED GLOVES IN COLLECTIONS

If, as well as knitting gloves, you would like to explore them further, there are dedicated collections of gloves, and there are collections that include gloves, both in the UK and around the world. Some collections can be visited 'in real life', but many are increasingly available on-line, which can be the most wonderful way to see items that would otherwise be impossible to view.

This chapter gives a pointer towards some of the collections that might be visited 'in real life', and also to those that have on-line collections that can be visited from anywhere in the world with access to a mobile phone or device and a good signal. The real-life collections and displays at the Dales Countryside Museum, the Tolbooth Sanquhar and Dumfries Museum in the UK have been mentioned in Chapters 2 and 3, and their contact details are given in the Resources section at the end of the book. However, there are several important collections on-line, details of which are given at the end of this section. The Glove Collection Trust has a large collection, an estimated 95 per cent of which is on-line and a good place to start.

The Glove Collection Trust

The Glove Collection Trust (GCT) is a body with close links to the Worshipful Company of Glovers of London, one of that city's ancient livery companies. Founded in 1349 and still going strong in the twenty-first century, the Glovers have a strong remit for charitable works. This section examines a small selection of knitted gloves in the electronic catalogue of the GCT.

The GCT, managed by a board of trustees, has over 2,000 items, the vast bulk of which are in the digital collection. The collection was kept for some years by the Fashion Museum in Bath, where the gloves were available for study by prior arrangement. Some were used in exhibitions on occasion. However, at the time of writing, the Fashion Museum is in the process of moving, and its collections are not accessible.

The GCT includes gloves and hand coverings of all types, including those made of leather and fabric. Knitted gloves are only a part of the Collection, which includes twelve pairs of liturgical gloves and two single liturgical gloves, some of which were discussed in Chapter 2. The liturgical gloves in the GCT collection are in the Holy Hands database and can be seen via that resource on the Knitting in Early Modern Europe (KEME) website, or through the GCT collection itself on its website; both links are in the Resources section at the back of the book.

When going into the Glove Collection Trust on-line, it's a good idea to have a general browse to get a sense of what is there. To look at knitted gloves there is a search facility that enables search terms to be entered: when using this, 'knitted' will yield results but 'knitting' will not.

There is also a search facility called 'Categories', and 'knitted' may be selected there, which will show a good selection. However, when referring to knitting, many of the Glove Collection Trust gloves are either fine frame or machine knitted, or they are finely knitted fabrics made into gloves like any other material, even using similar methods to those for making leather or skin gloves.

Given that the selection is so huge, here are some highlights that will be of interest to the hand knitter. Do look at the additional images on the website as you read about them. The level of detail is amazing, and in some respects can be better than actually seeing the gloves in real life. Certainly, as far as time goes, being able to study objects on-line with high quality photography is a big bonus.

The gloves selected are presented in date order, with the oldest dated items first. Just remember that dating textiles is a hazardous business! Do read this section with internet access to hand: even on a phone screen these gloves are inspirational.

Ecclesiastical Gloves, GCT 23400

Described as 'ecclesiastical gloves', these are not quite the same as the 'liturgical gloves' seen in Chapter 2. They were worn by nuns or abbesses, and are similar to fashionable gloves of the period. These wonderful long gloves would reach up the arm of the wearer, as they are 35cm (13.75in) from the fingertip to the cuff. They are hand knitted in silk and gold thread, with patterns of trees or flowers and stylised 'beasts'. The GCT gives their approximate date as between 1675 and 1699. The knitting is extremely fine, an approximate gauge being 100 stitches per 10cm (25 stitches per 1in), and 120 rows per 10cm (30 rows per 1in).

They are damaged in places: the decorative braid round the bottom edge is missing in the right glove, while the tip of the thumb on the same hand is also missing.

The fingers are especially interesting. Although they are plain with only lines of gold worked up their lengths, the thumb and first two fingers of both hands have vertical slits in them at their tips. In fact, the tip of the right thumb is missing altogether, perhaps because the vertical slit weakened it?

These gloves most likely belonged to a woman who was important in the church, the slits perhaps allowing rosary beads to be used while wearing them. They are similar in size and materials to two pairs that belonged to abbesses from a convent in Prague, in the Czech Republic. The Prague gloves have been studied and documented by Sylvie Odstrčilová in

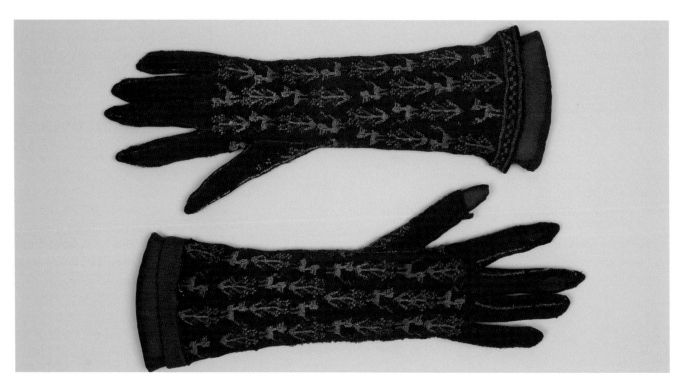

Ecclesiastical gloves from the Glove Collection Trust, GCT 23400. (© The Trustees of the Glove Collection Trust Fund. Reproduction of the image is with permission of the Trustees of the Glove Collection Trust and the Worshipful Company of Glovers of London)

Archaeological Textiles Review, Number 62 (*see* Bibliography). However, the pair in the GCT is richly patterned with gold-worked symbols, while both pairs in Prague are almost plain throughout.

These gloves came to the Glove Collection Trust having been part of the Spence Collection of gloves. Robert Spence (1871–1965) had worked as an artist and illustrator throughout his life, apart from distinguished service in a Quaker ambulance unit in World War I. It was perhaps from his professional work illustrating operas that his interest in costume, and therefore gloves, developed. His donation, made in 1959, was of 125 pairs, many of them decorative. There is more about Robert Spence on the GCT website (*see* link in Bibliography).

Available at https://theglovecollection.uk/?s=23400

Men's Gloves, GCT 2016.5

Knitted in an all-over pattern of lace, these gloves are a beautiful example of the knitter's art. Dated between 1700 and 1780, the pair is almost contemporary with the gloves that were found with Gunnister Man (*see* Chapter 2). However, they are different: they are cotton rather than wool, and in construction they are open work, and not a dense fabric. At this time, during the eighteenth century, cotton would have been imported in increasing quantities, and seen as a new and desirable fibre. Being in white cotton and in such an intricate lacy pattern, these gloves would surely have been a status symbol for their wearer.

Available at https://theglovecollection.uk/gloves/gct-2016-5/

Ecclesiastical Gloves, GCT 23414

These precisely dated gloves, 1768, are amongst the loveliest knitted liturgical gloves in the Glove Collection Trust. They also have some unusual features. Blue is not a colour often found in this type of glove, as they were usually white, red or green, later examples being in the colours of vestments for the appropriate part of the liturgical year. However, there is an association of blue with the Virgin Mary, so it could be that they were made for a particular place or person with that connection. Or perhaps the blue is in fact a faded green, which was a recognized colour for liturgical gloves?

These gloves represent the height of the hand-knitter's skill. Made in fine silk that has been plied, the tension or

Menswear gloves, GCT 2016.5. (© The Trustees of the Glove Collection Trust Fund. Reproduction of the image is with permission of the Trustees of the Glove Collection Trust and the Worshipful Company of Glovers of London)

gauge is approximately 70 stitches to 10cm (about 18 stitches to 1in). They are beautifully constructed with small gussets at the base of the fingers and a diamond of purl stitches at the base of the thumbs. The gloves were knitted flat in the hand sections and seamed up the side, but the fingers were knitted in the round. The embroidery is worked in metallic thread, and the cuffs are trimmed with bobbin lace made from silver thread. The gauntlets and the back of the hand with the embroidery are lined with silk fabric. The pointed fingers are another distinguishing feature, the pair in Chapter 2 using the same method for decreasing the tips! Their overall length is 27cm (10.5in), and they were part of the Spence Collection donated to the GCT in 1959.

Available at https://theglovecollection.uk/?s=23414

Womenswear Bead-Embroidered Gloves, GCT 23422

Dated between 1840 and 1849, this pair of gloves is covered with patterns of leaves and flowers in at least seven colours of beads knitted into the fabric on the backs of the hands

and up the fingers. The patterns surround the initials of the owner – perhaps the person who ordered them to be made? This work is most likely that of a professional workshop, as the skill required to make this artefact is enormous, the beads having to be threaded on to the knitting yarn before the work starts. The correct appearance of the pattern depends on the beads being threaded on to the knitting yarn in the order they are needed for the pattern.

The gloves themselves are cotton, and they measure 23cm (9in) in length. These gloves are fascinating in themselves, but even more interesting is the fact that there is an almost identical pair in the collection of the Centre de Documentacio i Museu Tèxtil (CDMT) in Terrassa, near Barcelona. The pair in the CDMT collection is dated 1850–60, they are cotton, they have initials worked in the same style of copperplate writing, one on the back of each hand, and are a little longer than the GCT pair at 24cm. The beads are in six colours, and are said to be of metal and glass. These were in an exhibition in 1997, and in the accompanying catalogue the gauge or tension is given as 60 stitches per 10cm (15 stitches per 1in), and 80 rounds per 10cm (20 rounds per 1in).

Womenswear bead-embroidered gloves, GCT 23422. (© The Trustees of the Glove Collection Trust Fund. Reproduction of the image is with permission of the Trustees of the Glove Collection Trust and the Worshipful Company of Glovers of London)

Womenswear knitted gloves, GCT 2017.67. (© The Trustees of the Glove Collection Trust Fund. Reproduction of the image is with permission of the Trustees of the Glove Collection Trust and the Worshipful Company of Glovers of London)

Other similarities between the two pairs include the cuff edge, a narrow band of rib with picot holes above, and the thumb construction, the shaping being delineated with lace holes.

This leads to numerous questions: where were they made? Are they the product of a professional workshop? Whose are the initials on each of them? The GCT pair has 'unknown' against 'Design/Manufacturer/Retailer', while the Terrassa pair came to their collection through the donation of Lluìs Giralt Tolosa of Barcelona (1905–1973), who had a personal textile collection, perhaps rather similar to that of Robert Spence?

The drawing at the beginning of the chapter imagines the two gloves being studied together, the pair in the Centre de Documentació i Museu Tèxtil (CDMT), Terrassa, Spain, via the on-line resource on the screen of a tablet, and the other 'in real life' in a study room in the UK.

Available at https://theglovecollection.uk/?s=23422

Womenswear Knitted Gloves, GCT 2017.67

These look like a pair of woolly gloves from the 1960s that might be found with the winter hats and scarves in a hall cupboard: slightly fluffy, a little worn, with fur round the cuffs, which is a cosy feature. So why is this pair in the GCT? As is so often the case with gloves (and indeed with many 'everyday' objects), it's not necessarily the gloves themselves, but their associations. This pair is recorded as having belonged to, and been worn by Elsa Schiaparelli, the fashion designer responsible for the colour 'shocking pink' and a hat shaped like a shoe, designed in collaboration with Salvador Dali in 1937–8. This is how a relatively unexceptional pair of gloves gains a place in glove history due to its associations.

Available at https://theglovecollection.uk/?s=2017.67

Knitted Gloves, GCT 2012.7.7

This pair, obviously unworn, and obviously hand knitted, appeared in an exhibition at the Fashion Museum, Bath, in 2019–20. The gloves were shown alongside a pair of finely knitted silk mittens and an ornately patterned pair of gloves (this is the pair at the back of the illustration that opens Chapter 2 (GCT 23415)). In the 2019–20 exhibition, under the title *Where East Meets West*, the caption draws links between these items. The two historic pairs on display show the carnation as a design symbol, often used in Ottoman textiles from the Middle East, while the hand-knitted gloves came from Syria, the same region.

Dated as made in 2004, these gloves are striking in their use of bright red for the fingertips, contrasting sharply with the white of the fingers. The thumb construction is worth a look: it appears to be a peasant thumb, but set slightly to the side of the hand, rather than on the palm.

Available at https://theglovecollection.uk/?s=2012.7.7

Knitted gloves, GCT 2012.7.7. (© The Trustees of the Glove Collection Trust Fund. Reproduction of the image is with permission of the Trustees of the Glove Collection Trust and the Worshipful Company of Glovers of London)

Exploring Collections On-line

The Covid-19 pandemic restricted movement from March 2020 in the UK and elsewhere, which meant that travel of any sort was abruptly curtailed, including visiting museums and galleries to study gloves. It proved to be the prompt for doing research on-line, instead of 'in real life'. As the recipient of a research grant at this time, part of which was intended to fund travel to collections, extensive use was made of on-line catalogues. This is the basis for the following listing of on-line resources – which does not, however, claim to be complete or definitive: it is just a taster of what I discovered! It will also be found that not all the websites work at all times. Search engines can be especially temperamental, not always throwing up the same results despite search terms being the same. This seems to be a feature of museum and collection search engines.

The Worshipful Company of Glovers: https://www.thegloverscompany.org/ gives an insight into the work of this ancient organization, and a link to the collection on-line.

The Glove Collection Trust: https://theglovecollection.uk/ Some examples have been selected from this collection and have been discussed earlier in this chapter. The collection is shown to its best advantage, with high quality images including many details.

Knitting in Early Modern Europe: https://kemeresearch.com/ Mentioned in Chapter 2, a sign-in is required; following that, the site is free to access and contains the database of liturgical gloves developed by the 'Holy Hands' project.

Centre de Documentació i Museu Tèxtil: This centre has a catalogue and database of their collections called IMATEX: https://cdmt.cat/en/textilteca/

Boston Museum of Fine Arts: https://www.mfa.org/collections The textiles collection has about 200 gloves, including over a dozen knitted silk liturgical and non-liturgical gloves. The quality of the images is excellent, making for good browsing.

The Future Museum, South West Scotland: This is an on-line partnership between several local authorities and museums, including the Tolbooth Museum Sanquhar, and Dumfries Museum, both of which have Sanquhar gloves and associated exhibits. These are available on-line under Collections/Life & Work/Key Industries/Textiles/Sanquhar Knitting:

http://futuremuseum.co.uk/collections/life-work/key-industries/textiles/sanquhar-knitting.aspx
Many examples of vintage Sanquhar gloves are shown.

Estonian National Museums: Glove collections are available on-line via the public portal: https://www.muis.ee/en_GB/search

Search 'kinnas' or 'kindad', which are Estonian for 'glove' or 'gloves'.

The Collection of the Knitting & Crochet Guild

The next group of gloves are from the collection of the Knitting & Crochet Guild (KCG). Some of the colour-patterned gloves from this collection have been seen already in Chapter 3, as among these there is a pair of Dales gloves and some Sanquhar gloves.

However, these are not the only gloves in the KCG Collection. There are more knitted gloves, and some are now shown. At the time of writing, only a small part of the KCG Collection is available on-line; however, a project is underway to make more of the collection available digitally.

Each pair is described as documented on the KCG database, and the accession number is included. They are discussed in an order that reflects their complexity.

Classic Hand-Knitted Gloves

These gloves are knitted in stocking stitch, in green wool, and are 24cm (9.5in) long.

This pair of gloves is perfectly knitted by hand in wool, in the round. A classic of their type, they were part of a bequest from the estate of a Mrs Kitchen. Given after her death, it included a large number of very beautifully knitted and crocheted pieces. The vast majority of the KCG Collection has come from the relatives and friends of the members of the Guild, along with some pieces bought from specialist dealers,

Classic hand-knitted gloves.

Wool gloves knitted sideways.

such as we saw with the Dales gloves in Chapter 3. Having come into being in this way, much of the KCG Collection represents what 'ordinary' women were making at home in the twentieth century. The levels of skill and manufacture are often exemplary.

However, Mrs Kitchen, the knitter of these gloves, was in a stellar category because documents that came with the donation of her textiles show that she was active in the Women's Institute in Derbyshire from the mid-1950s, having work selected for exhibitions and often winning full marks for the skill shown in their making. Mrs Kitchen was also a skilled needlewoman and maker of crochet.

Wool Gloves Knitted Sideways

These gloves are knitted sideways with the seam up the outside of the hand. The rib welt is worked downwards. They are from the Audrie Stratford donation (1991.004.0001) – *see* below.

Knitting a glove sideways seems to be a way to maximize the effort and amount of sewing up that has to be done after the knitting, whether this is actual sewing of seams, or some sort of grafting, having used provisional cast-ons. These firmly knitted wool gloves use short rows to shape the hands, and the rib was knitted down from them, having been picked up from the side edge of the knitting. As an example of glove construction, they are interesting: patterns can be found for

Short rows used to shape the thumb on sideways-knitted gloves.

sideways-knitted gloves on the knitting machine, as well as the garter-stitch pair designed by Elizabeth Zimmermann, mentioned in Chapter 1.

These gloves represent a part of the first donation made to the KCG Collection by the late Audrie Stratford at the time of its founding in 1991. A knitter and writer herself, Audrie Stratford collected a large number of items as a foundation for the collection, including the Norwegian patterned gloves and the 'ID' single Sanquhar glove, both seen in Chapter 3. According to the record, these sideways gloves were knitted by Audrie herself.

Audrie was the author of several books in the 1970s and 1980s: *Introducing Knitting*, *Nowadays Knitting for New Knitters*, and *Better Knitting Made Easier for Blind People*. She was fascinated by structure and techniques, and experimented widely with hand knitting: a very useful piece, now in the collection, is a strip of stocking-stitch fabric that she knitted, in medium-weight wool knitted using every size of knitting needle from the finest to the thickest, the same number of rows with each size of needle – a crash course in the relationship between yarn, needle size and gauge or tension!

Heritage Collection Gansey-style Gloves

These gloves are from the Heritage Collection project, Kit 8 (2021.011.0001A and B).

This pair was designed and knitted by a KCG member in 1997 as part of a scheme to provide kits inspired by pieces from the collection, for sale to raise funds for the Guild. There were about twenty in all, of which this was one. Firmly knitted in an authentic 5-ply Guernsey wool, the pattern specifies a set of 2.25mm needles, giving a hard-wearing and close fabric. The lower edge is cast on using the Channel Islands style, which uses a thumb method and the yarn doubled, producing a knotted edge.

The written instructions in the paper pattern leaflet take up about a page of text explaining how to do this; now, of course, it's possible to go on the internet for instructional videos to learn new techniques! The cables and moss-stitch panels reference the patterns used in traditional Guernseys – or 'Ganseys' – but the pattern writer, designer and knitter states at the start: 'Although these gloves use traditional stitches and stitch patterns, they are in no way authentic and are a new design incorporating old ideas.'

The stitch patterns are carefully placed, a cable running up the thumb, the second and fourth fingers, while the first and third fingers have a continuation of the moss-stitch panels. The palm is plain stocking stitch.

The pattern instructions have the thumb being knitted on completion of the increases for it. This method means that the glove can be tried on with the thumb complete, which makes gauging the depth of the hand easier before the hand and fingers are started.

The 'old ideas' certainly translate well into gloves. These would last a lifetime.

Gloves Knitted Flat with a Gauntlet

These gloves are knitted in stocking stitch with two colour patterns on a flared wrist, in dark red with pink (2004.060.0017 A & B).

Knitted in a firm, highly twisted wool, the fabric is close enough for the gauntlets to hold their shape without

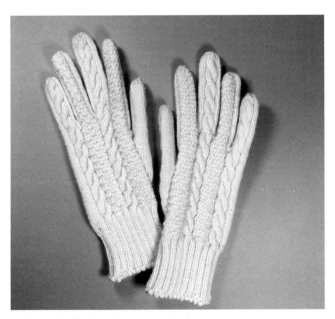

Heritage Collection Gansey-style gloves.

Gloves knitted flat with a gauntlet.

any lining. The simple two-colour design around the gauntlet suggests they are perhaps from the 1950s. With the exception of those knitted sideways and therefore flat (mentioned earlier in this section), they are the only gloves in this book that have been knitted on two needles and seamed. There are seams running up the sides of the hands and up every finger. The thumb gusset is very clearly shaped, with symmetrical increases showing clearly in the tightly spun wool.

These gloves were part of a donation to the KCG Collection by Sue Leighton-White in 2004, and they have a co-incidental connection to other gloves in this book. Sue was the researcher and author who studied Mary Allen's gloves in the Wordsworth Museum, and who published her findings and pattern for a replica pair in *Piecework* magazine in 1994, reprinted in *Knitting Traditions* in 2012.

Ringwood-type Glove

In these gloves the fingers are in stocking stitch, in a pale yellow cotton (1997.123.0001).

This sample of gloves from the KCG Collection finishes with two pairs of 'Ringwood'-style gloves. Both are hand knitted, in light yellow cotton, and use a textured pattern.

The first pair came into the collection in 1997 from the ninety-two-year-old great aunt of the donor. It is not clear if they were domestically knitted, as the documentation states that there are 'Yellow gloves sold in Dorset as riding gloves', but not necessarily this pair. They use a broken rib for the hand, and the fingers are knitted in stocking stitch. They have been worn, as there are some stray threads from the bottom of the fingers and thumbs.

The cast-on appears to be a tubular method, similar to that produced on a knitting machine, which was extremely unusual in hand knitting at that time, and which might indicate that this pair was made in a workshop or had a professional origin. This is a great cast-on for gloves as it is stretchy and therefore good for cotton yarn, which has no stretch. There are videos giving instructions for the cast-on – the link is provided in the Resources section at the back of the book.

The thumbs are a simple peasant thumb, unlike the authentic Ringwood gloves, which have a shaped gusset thumb. The speed and simplicity of the peasant thumb method might also indicate that these were knitted for sale. We will probably never know how this pair came into being!

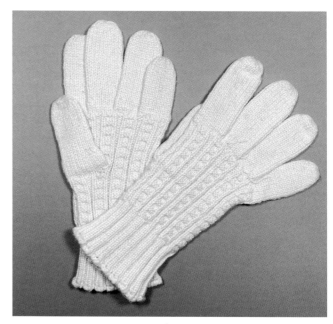

Ringwood-type glove.

Tubular cast-on of a Ringwood-style glove.

Ringwood Gloves by Dent's

These gloves are of light yellow cotton, and are an example of a commercially made Ringwood-type glove. They are labelled 'Dent's Real Hand Knit Gloves', are dated from the 1950s, and are unworn; they are priced at £8 (2012.000.0025) – *see* below.

The KCG Collection has as its focus domestically made hand and machine knitting and crochet, but the distinction

Ringwood gloves by Dent's.

The Dent's label.

is not always easy to make, as is the case with this example. Ringwood is a small town in Hampshire, England, and Ringwood gloves were knitted at home by people who were paid by the pair for their work. It's not clear from the catalogue entry whether they were £8 in cost, or whether they were bought for the collection for £8! They are unworn as they still have their paper label on them, which reads 'Dent's Real Hand Knit Gloves', together with 'Made in England' in much smaller print at the bottom.

These gloves have no connection, however, with Dent village in the Yorkshire Dales. As we saw in Chapter 3, there were wool gloves produced in Dent, which was also the home of the 'terrible knitters', and later of Mary Allen and her glove-knitting mother. The Dent here, however, is a commercial firm that makes gloves, still in business now, with a factory in Warminster, a town in the southern English county of Wiltshire.

Ringwood gloves have been thoroughly documented by Richard Rutt in *A History of Hand Knitting*, where he gives an account of this trade, including a picture of a pair of Ringwood gloves knitted in 1985 by Beatrice Dennis of Ringwood. The pair from the KCG Collection and pictured here is recognizably similar in stitch pattern and construction to those illustrated and knitted in Ringwood.

They are knitted in a mercerized cotton in the round; in fact a line can be seen up the back of the right hand

suggesting where the stitches fell on the double-pointed needles that were most likely used to knit these. The knitting is not especially fine, at a tension or gauge of about 28 stitches to 10cm (7 stitches to 1in).

Richard Rutt points out that patterns were published for these gloves, and prints the (very minimal) instructions for the true Ringwood glove. Perhaps the earliest of this type was the 'Gentleman's Warm Glove', which was issued in a 1910 booklet, *J & J Baldwin's Penny Guide to Knitting & Crochet*, subtitled *A book of practical instruction of the use of knitting wools in the production by hand of serviceable garments for every-daywear*. However, these were not exactly the same as the real Ringwood pattern, which is two rounds plain and one round knit one purl one rib.

The firms of Baldwins and Patons were merged by 1916, when the pattern was published again in the Patons & Baldwins publication *Woolcraft* (1916). However, by the 13th edition the pattern had been replaced by a plain pair of gloves for men. In the 1930s, Twilleys, the cotton yarn spinners, published patterns for knitted cotton gloves with similar patterns, and specified 'glove cotton' as the yarn.

The pattern that follows here is for a textured glove, and is adapted from these patterns. The fit, shape and size are more suitable to modern hands, and the instructions are given more fully than in the originals from over a century ago.

Pattern 6: Vintage Inspiration

Modelled on Ringwood and similar textured gloves in the previous section, this is a great stitch pattern for a plain coloured glove as the texture gives extra warmth and increased grip. These gloves could be knitted in wool or cotton, the Ringwood gloves in pale yellow cotton being a classic for country wear and riding.

The double knitting yarn gives a large glove while the 4-ply yarn gives a smaller pair using the same instructions, depending on which yarn weight is chosen. Obviously some measurements differ, such as the finger lengths. The decreasing for the finger tips adds about 6mm (0.25in) to the length. The textured pattern does not fit around all the fingers exactly but place a marker at the start of the round and continue it from the hands and any discrepancies will be at the side of the fingers. The thumb shaping for these gloves is easier to follow from a chart that shows the position of the increases and the textured pattern. However, written out instructions are also given.

Pattern 6: 'Vintage Inspiration', in Woodland DK in dyed Frost.

The thumb shaping of the smaller glove in Woodland 4-ply dyed Lichen.

Materials

Yarn

Blacker Yarns, Woodland DK (large/men's gloves), 100% British wool, 100g skein, 210m/229yds colour dyed Frost, 1 skein.
Finished DK gloves weigh 95g and take 199m/217yds approx.

Blacker Yarns, Woodland 4-ply (medium/ladies' gloves), 100% British wool, 100g skein 320m/350yds, colour dyed Lichen, 1 skein.
Finished 4-ply gloves weigh 62g and take 200m/218 yds approx.

Needles

3.75mm (DK) or 3.25mm (4-ply) knitting needles or size to achieve gauge (*see* Chapter 1 for type of knitting needles).

Tools

Stitch markers or lengths of contrasting yarn tied into loops.
Stitch holders and/or lengths of smooth strong contrasting yarn for holding stitches.
Wool sewing needle and scissors for finishing.

Finished size:

Measurements are flexible as there is so much texture in the gloves.

DK:
- Length: 28cm/11in.
- All round above thumb: 20cm/8in.

4-ply:
- Length: 23cm/9in.
- All round above thumb: 19cm/7.5in.

Tension/gauge:

DK: 22 sts x 32 rounds = 10cm/4in square over seed stitch knitted in the round.

4-ply: 26 sts x 36 rounds = 10 cm/4in square over seed stitch knitted in the round.

Abbreviations:

See abbreviations list at back of book.

Special techniques:

See 'Techniques for knitting plain gloves' in Chapter 1.
Note: thumb shaping is asymmetrical.
Thumb is knitted before fingers.

Special stitch:
Seed stitch (multiple of 4 sts)

Rnd 1: *k1, p1, k2; rep from * to end.
Rnd 2: k.
Rnd 3: *k3, p1; rep from * to end.
Rnd 4: k.
Rep rnd 1–4 for pattern.

Instructions

Note: use DK for larger gloves and 4-ply for a smaller pair.

Right Glove

CO 48 sts using appropriate yarn and needles. Join for working in the round.
PM for start of round if wanted, checking sts are not twisted.
Work in K2 P2 rib (k2, p2) around), for 20 rnds. DK 8cm/3in. 4-ply 5cm/2in.
Next round: (k1f&b, K23) 2 times. 50 sts **.

Thumb gusset:

NB: the chart shows the thumb and the first 5 sts of the round.

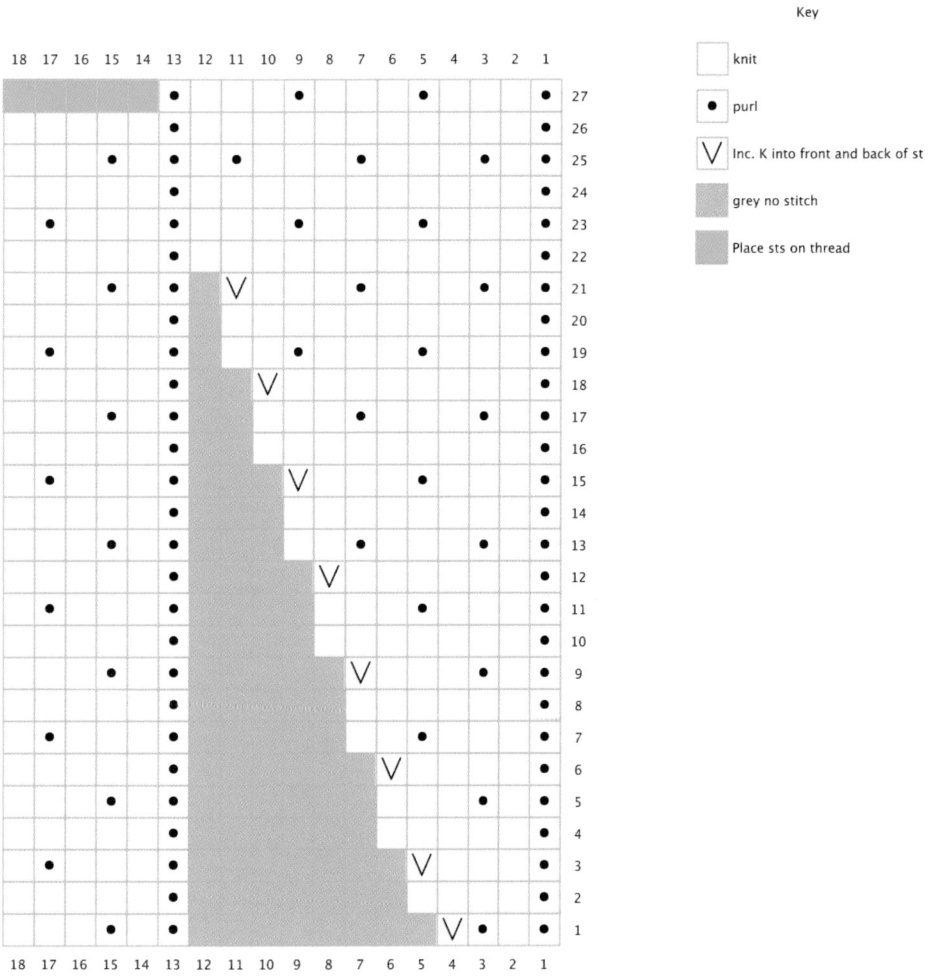

Key

(blank)	knit
●	purl
V	Inc. K into front and back of st
(light grey)	grey no stitch
(dark grey)	Place sts on thread

18	17	16	15	14	13	12	11	10	9	8	7	6	5	4	3	2	1	Rnd
▨	▨	▨	▨	▨	●				●				●				●	27
					●												●	26
			●		●		●				●				●		●	25
					●												●	24
	●				●				●				●				●	23
					●												●	22
			●		●	▒	V				●				●		●	21
					●	▒	▒										●	20
	●				●	▒	▒		●				●				●	19
					●	▒	▒	V									●	18
			●		●	▒	▒	▒			●				●		●	17
					●	▒	▒	▒									●	16
	●				●	▒	▒	▒	V				●				●	15
					●	▒	▒	▒	▒								●	14
			●		●	▒	▒	▒	▒	●					●		●	13
					●	▒	▒	▒	▒	V							●	12
	●				●	▒	▒	▒	▒	▒			●				●	11
					●	▒	▒	▒	▒	▒							●	10
			●		●	▒	▒	▒	▒	▒	V				●		●	9
					●	▒	▒	▒	▒	▒	▒						●	8
	●				●	▒	▒	▒	▒	▒	▒		●				●	7
					●	▒	▒	▒	▒	▒	▒	V					●	6
			●		●	▒	▒	▒	▒	▒	▒	▒	▒		●		●	5
					●	▒	▒	▒	▒	▒	▒	▒	▒				●	4
	●				●	▒	▒	▒	▒	▒	▒	▒	▒	V			●	3
					●	▒	▒	▒	▒	▒	▒	▒	▒				●	2
			●		●	▒	▒	▒	▒	▒	▒	▒	▒	V	●		●	1
18	17	16	15	14	13	12	11	10	9	8	7	6	5	4	3	2	1	

Pattern 6: right thumb.

Either follow the chart *or* the written instructions here:

Rnd 1: P1, K1, P1, K1f&b, P1, PM, work rnd 1 of seed stitch pattern to last st, K1; 51 sts.

Rnd 2: P1, K4, P1, SLM, K to end of rnd.

Rnd 3: P1, K3, P1, K1f&b, P1, SLM, work rnd 3 of seed stitch pattern to last st, K1; 52 sts.

Rnd 4: P1, K5, P1, SLM, K to end of rnd.

Inc Rnd 5: P1, work in seed stitch pattern to 2 sts before marker, K1f&b, P1, SLM, work in seed stitch pattern to last st, K1; 53 sts.

Work 2 rnds in pattern.

Working new sts into seed stitch pattern, rep last 3 rnds 5 more times; 58 sts.

Work 4 rnds in pattern.

Knit thumb:

Work 13 sts in pattern, place rem 45 sts onto a length of contrast yarn, CO 5 sts, 18 sts remain for thumb. Work in the rnd in seed stitch pattern until thumb measures 4.5 (5.5) cm/1.75 (2.25) in, or length required, ending with a K rnd.

Key

☐ knit

● purl

V Inc. K into front and back of st

▨ grey no stitch

▨ Place sts onto thread

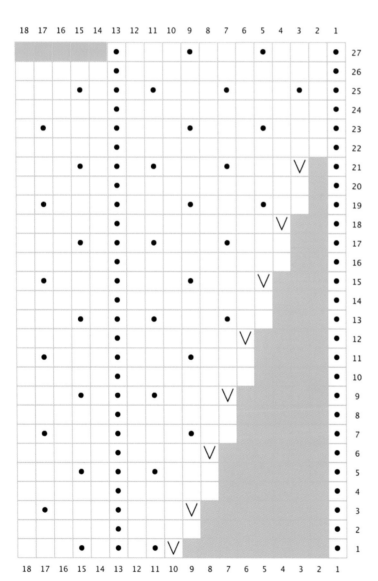

Pattern 6: left thumb.

Shape thumb:
Shape tip:
Next round: K1, k2tog all round. 12 sts.
Next round: K.
Next round: K2tog 6 times; 6 sts.
Cut yarn, draw through sts, tighten and fasten off.

Hand:
PUK 3 sts from thumb CO, return the 45 sts on contrast yarn to needles and work in pattern to end of rnd; 48 sts.
Work in seed stitch pattern for 14 rnds or desired length to base of fingers.

First finger:
Work 4 sts in pattern, place next 34 sts onto a length of contrast yarn, CO 2 sts, work 10 sts in pattern; 16 sts.
Work in the rnd in seed stitch pattern until finger measures 4 (7) cm/2 (2.75) in, or length required, ending with a k rnd.

Shape tip:
Next round: K1, K2tog all round to last st, K1; 11 sts.
Next round: K.
Next round: K2tog around, to last st, K1; 6 sts.
Finish as for thumb

Second finger:
Return first and last 6 sts from contrast yarn onto needles.
Next round: Work 6 sts in pattern, CO 2 sts, work 6 sts in pattern, PUK 3 sts from first finger; 17 sts.
Work in the rnd in seed stitch pattern until finger measures 5.5 (7.5) cm/2.25 (3) in or length required ending with a k rnd.

Shape tip:
Next round: K1, K2tog round to last 2 sts, K2; 12 sts.
Next round: K.
Next round: K2tog around; 6 sts.
Finish as for thumb

Third finger:
Return first and last 6 sts from contrast yarn onto needles.
Next round: Work 6 sts in pattern, CO 2 sts, work 6 sts in pattern, PUK 2 sts from second finger; 16 sts.
Work in the rnd in seed stitch pattern until finger measures 5 (7) cm/2 (2.75) in or length required ending with a k rnd.
Shape tip and finish as first finger.

Fourth finger:
Place remaining 10 sts from contrast yarn onto needles, Rejoin yarn.
Work 10 sts in pattern, PUK 4 sts from base of third finger; 14 sts.
Join for working in the round and work in pattern until finger measures 4.5 (5.5) cm/1.75 (2.25) in or until length required ending with a K rnd.

Shape tip:
Next round: K1, K2tog 4 times, K2; 10 sts.
Next round: K.
Next round: K2tog 5 times; 5 sts.
Finish as for thumb.

Left Glove

Work as right glove to **
Start shaping thumb gusset:
Note: the chart shows the thumb and the first 5 sts of the round.

Either follow the chart *or* the written instructions here:

Rnd 1: P1, K1f&b, P1, K1, P1, PM, work rnd 1 of seed stitch pattern to last st, K1; 51 sts.
Rnd 2: P1, K4, P1, SLM, K to end of rnd.
Rnd 3: P1, K1f&b, K3, P1, SLM, work rnd 3 of seed stitch pattern to last st, K1; 52 sts.
Rnd 4: P1, K5, P1, SLM, K to end of rnd.
Inc Rnd 5: P1, K1f&b, work in seed stitch pattern to 1 st before marker, P1, SLM, work in seed stitch pattern to last st, K1; 53 sts.
Work 2 rnds in pattern.
Working new sts into seed stitch pattern, rep last 3 rnds 5 more times; 58 sts.
Work 4 rnds in pattern.

Thumb:
Work as for right glove.

Hand:
Return the 45 sts on length of yarn to needles and join yarn.
Work 45 sts in pattern, PUK 3 sts from base of thumb; 48 sts.

Work in the rnd in seed stitch pattern for 14 rnds or desired length to base of fingers.

First finger:
Work 10 sts in pattern, place next 34 sts onto a length of contrast yarn, CO 2 sts, work 4 sts in pattern; 16 sts.
Finish as for first finger of right glove.

Second, third, and fourth fingers
Work as for right glove.

Finishing:
Darn in all ends, closing any gaps at the base of the fingers as necessary. Give the gloves a light press with a hot iron and damp cloth or according to instructions given with the yarn.

Pattern 6: 'Vintage Inspiration' gloves in Woodland 4 ply, dyed Lichen

APPENDIX I: ABBREVIATIONS

alt	alternate		m	metres
approx.	approximately		MC	main colour
CC	contrast colour		P/p	purl
CO	cast on using preferred method		PM	place marker
cm	centimetres		PUK	pick up and knit
dec	decrease(d)		rep	repeat
dpns	double-pointed needles		rnd(s)	round(s)
g	grams		sl	slip
in	inches		SLM	slip marker
inc	increase(d)		ssk	slip each of the next two stitches (as if to knit) independently, return them to the left needles and knit through the back loops
K/k	knit			
K1f&b	knit into the front & the back of the stitch			
K2tog	knit 2 sts together		st(s)	stitch(es)
K3tog	knit 3 sts together		tbl	through back of loops
M1L	pick up bar between stitches from front to back and knit into the back		tog	together
			yd	yards
M1R	pick up bar between stitches from back to front, place on left needle and knit into front			

APPENDIX II: ALPHABET CHARTS

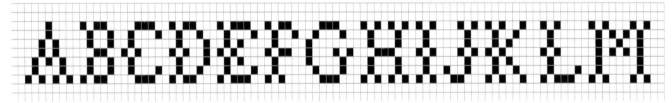

Alphabet A–M.

Alphabet N–Z.

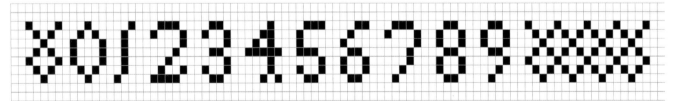

Numbers and motifs.

BIBLIOGRAPHY

Books

Beck, S.W., *Gloves, their Annals and Associations: A Chapter of Trade and Social History* (Hamilton, Adams & Co., 1883).

Budd, A., *The Knitter's Handy Book of Patterns: Basic Designs in Multiple Sizes and Gauges* (Interweave Press, 2002).

Bush, N., *Folk Knitting in Estonia: A Garland of Symbolism, Tradition and Technique* (Interweave Press, 1999).

Coatsworth, E., and Owen-Crocker, G., *Clothing the Past: Surviving Garments from Early Medieval to Early Modern Western Europe* (Brill, 2018, Chapter 10).

Cumming, V., *Gloves* (Batsford, 1982).

Emlyn-Jones, G., *Glove Making: The Art and the Craft* (Lacis Publications, 2003).

Ford, F., *Knitsonik Stranded Colourwork Sourcebook* (Knitsonik publication, 2014).

Hartley, M., and Ingilby, J., *The Old Hand-Knitters of the Dales.* (Cooperative Press, 2014) NB New edition with foreword and pattern by Penelope Lister Hemingway.

Jõeste, K., and Ehin, K., *Ornamented Journey* (Saara Publishing House, 2012).

Patons Woolcraft (Patons & Baldwin, various edns).

Piiri, R., *Suur kindaraamat. Eesti kihelkondade mustrid* (Hea Lugu/Eesti Rahva Muuseum, 2013).

Pink, A., Reiman, S., and Jõeste, K., *Estonian Knitting 1: Traditions and Techniques* (Saara Publishing House, 2016).

Pink, A., *Estonian Knitting 2: Socks and Stockings* (Saara Publishing House, 2018).

Redwood, M., *Gloves and Glove-Making* (Shire Books, 2016).

Rutt, R., *A History of Hand Knitting* (Batsford, 1987).

Schoeser, M., *Rozanne Hawksley: Offerings* (Ruthin Craft Centre/Lund Humphries, 2009).

Smith, W., *Gloves: Past & Present* (The Sherwood Press Inc., 1917).

Stanley, M., *Knitter's Handbook* (various editions from 1986).

Thomas, M., *Mary Thomas's Knitting Book* (Hodder & Stoughton, 1938).

Turnau, I., *History of Knitting before Mass Production* (Institute of the History of Material Culture. Polish Academy of Sciences, 1991).

Willemsen, A., *Honderden ... Van hand tot hand. Handschoenen en wanten in de Nederlanden voor 1700* (SPA Publishers, 2015).

Zimmermann, E., *Knit One, Knit All* (Schoolhouse Press, 2011).

Articles and Papers

Batchelor, P., 'The Terrible Knitters of Dent', *The Knitter*, Issue 73 (June 2014 pp. 82–83).

Bush, N., 'The Symbolism of Gloves', *Knitting Traditions* (2010, pp. 58–59).

Carbonell, S., Gauntes episcopales con mensaje/ Episcopal gloves with a message, *Datatextil* 17 (2007, pp. 82–88) available at: https://raco.cat/index.php/Datatextil/article/view/276586/364544

Cardon, D., 'Les gants liturgiques du moyen âge et les origines de la maille en Europe', in *Trésors textiles du Moyen Âge en Languedoc-Rousillon*. Carcassonne (Musée des Beaux Arts de Carcassonne, 1993, pp. 29–39).

Hemingway, P., 'Sarah Hunter's Gloves', *The Knitter*, Issue 150 (April 2020, pp. 66–70).

Hemingway, P., 'Adder Back Gloves', *Yarn Forward*, 26 (July 2010).

Henshall, A. S., and Maxwell S., 'Clothing and Other Articles from a Late 17th-century Grave at Gunnister, Shetland', *Proceedings of the Antiquaries of Scotland (PSAS) 1951–1952. 86: 30–42* (1954).

Leighton-White, S., 'The Needles' Music: Hand Knitters of the Dales', *Piecework* (January–February 1994, pp. 56–62). NB no pattern included.

Leighton-White, S., 'The Needles' Music: Hand Knitters of the Dales', *Knitting Traditions* (Winter 2011, pp. 12–14).

Leighton-White, S., 'Mary Allen's Gloves', *Knitting Traditions* (Winter 2011, pp. 14–17). Instructions and charts for knitting a pair.

Odstrčilová, S., 'The So-Called St. Adalbert's Glove from Prague: An Early Example of a Knitted Liturgical Glove', *Piecework* (January–February 2016, pp. 8–12).

Odstrčilová, S., 'Pious Vanity: Two Pairs of 18th Century Abbesses' Knitted Gloves', *Archaeological Textiles Review*, 62 (2020, pp. 144–151).

Thomas, A., *Sanquhar Gloves: An Exemplification of Deep Local to Pan Global?* Textile Society of America Symposium Proceedings (2018).

Available at: https://digitalcommons.unl.edu/tsaconf/1116/

RESOURCES

On-Line Collections

The Glove Collection Trust: https://theglovecollection.uk/
Some examples have been selected from this collection and are discussed in Chapter 5. This collection is shown to its best advantage with high quality images including many details.

Booklet Giving the History of the Glove Collection Trust:
https://theglovecollection.uk/wp-content/uploads/2020/07/Douglas-Sweet-Booklet-Version-6-LATEST.pdf

Information About Robert Spence and His Glove Collection:
https://www.thegloverscompany.org/livery-archives-a-window-into-another-world/robert-spence-his-story

Rozanne Hawksley's Gloves: https://theglovecollection.uk/?s=rozanne
Accession numbers GCT 2020.1, GCT 2020.2, GCT 2020.3, GCT 2020.4, GCT 2020.5

The Worshipful Company of Glovers: https://www.thegloverscompany.org/
Gives an insight into the work of this ancient organization and a link to the collection on-line.

Knitting in Early Modern Europe: https://kemeresearch.com/

A sign-in is required; following that, the site is free to access and contains the database of liturgical gloves developed by the 'Holy Hands' project.

Victoria & Albert Museum Collection: https://www.vam.ac.uk/collections?type=featured
A rich source of knitted gloves. Search 'knitted gloves'; shows several mentioned in this book, specifically:
Liturgical gloves 437&A-1892: https://collections.vam.ac.uk/item/O107792/pair-of-gloves-unknown/
Gloves knitted in sea silk T.15-1926: https://collections.vam.ac.uk/item/O360663/pair-of-gloves/

Centre de Documentació i Museu Tèxtil: https://cdmt.cat/en/textilteca/
This centre has a catalogue and database of their collections called IMATEX.

Boston Museum of Fine Arts: https://www.mfa.org/collections
The textiles collection has about 200 gloves, including over a dozen knitted silk liturgical and non-liturgical gloves. The quality of the images is excellent, making for good browsing.

The Future Museum, South West Scotland: http://futuremuseum.co.uk/collections/life-work/key-industries/textiles/sanquhar-knitting.aspx
This is an on-line partnership between several local authorities and museums including the Tolbooth Museum and the

Sanquhar and Dumfries Museum, both of which have Sanquhar gloves and associated exhibits. These are available on-line under Collections > Life & Work > Key Industries > Textiles > Sanquhar Knitting.

Many examples of vintage Sanquhar gloves are shown.

Estonian National Museums: https://www.muis.ee/en_GB/search

Glove collections are available on-line via the public portal. Search 'kinnas' or 'kindad', which are Estonian for glove or gloves; or search using the accession numbers given in the text, Chapters 2 and 3.

Glove Knitting Information and Supplies

Dales Knitting

Ann Kingstone, Yorkshire Knitting:
These posts have useful information about Dales gloves from Ann's research:
https://annkingstone.com/where-did-mary-allen-live/2018
https://annkingstone.com/swaledale-gloves/2019
https://annkingstone.com/the-angela-glove/2020
https://annkingstone.com/the-terrible-knitters-of-dent/2021

Yorkshire Dales Gloves Interview Between Ann Kingstone and Angharad Thomas:
https://www.youtube.com/watch?v=HmN4LxF9eP4

Sanquhar Knitting

A' the Airts Community Art Centre and Café:
8–12 High Street,
Sanquhar,
DG4 6BL, United Kingdom.
https://atheairts.org.uk/

Supplies patterns and other Sanquhar items.

Stenhouse & Crafty Artists:
19–21 High Street,
Sanquhar,
Dumfriesshire,
DG4 6DJ,
United Kingdom.

Supplies patterns, needles and yarns.

Sanquhar Pattern Designs:
Sanquhar Pattern Designs,
8–12 High Street,
Sanquhar,
Dumfriesshire,
DG4 6BL,
United Kingdom.
https://www.sanquharknits.com/

Sanquhar knitwear and accessories.

EJT Knitting – Euro Japan Trading Co.:
https://www.ejtknitting.co.uk/SanquharGloves.html

Patterns and yarns for Sanquhar gloves and other items. Sanquhar 3-ply yarn: black or white 75 per cent wool/25 per cent nylon.

Knitting & Crochet Guild:
P & B pattern leaflet 87 available free for members and non-members. Contact:
collections@kcguild.org.uk.

Scottish Women's Institutes:
Scottish Women's Institutes sell patterns for Sanquhar gloves in four patterns: Prince of Wales, Duke, Midge and Flea, and Shepherd's Plaid.
https://shop.theswi.org.uk/products/swi-sanquhar-gloves-pattern

Interweave:
Sanquhar gloves with Beth Brown-Reinsel; video download:
https://www.interweave.com/product/sanquhar-gloves-video-download/

Ravelry Sanquhar Knitting Group:
https://www.ravelry.com/groups/sanquhar-knitting-group

Ringwood Gloves

Knitty, Issue 33, Deep Fall 2010:
Pattern available at:
https://knitty.com/ISSUEdf10/PATTringwood.php

Tubular Cast-on Like Yellow Gloves:
https://verypink.com/2019/04/10/tubular-cast-on-in-the-round/

On-line Resources

Alice Kettle:
https://alicekettle.co.uk/telling-fortunes/

Blacker Yarns:
All about yarn.
https://www.blackeryarns.co.uk/advice-information/all-about-yarn/

Brooklyn Tweed Lookbooks:
https://brooklyntweed.com/pages/lookbooks

Brooklyn Tweed Videos:
How it's made: Woollen-Spun Yarn.
https://brooklyntweed.com/pages/a-video-library

How it's made: Worsted-Spun Yarn:
https://brooklyntweed.com/pages/a-video-library

Canva.com:
Useful for making moodboards.
https://www.canva.com/about/
https://www.canva.com/learn/make-a-mood-board

Framework Knitters Guild:
https://www.frameworkknitters.co.uk/

Freddie Robins:
Hands of Hoxton.
http://freddierobins.com/pre-2000.php

Fibre Nation: Gunnister Man Podcast:
https://www.interweave.com/fiber-nation/gunnister-man-mystery/

Knit Companion:
App for tracking knitting in progress.
https://www.knitcompanion.com/

Knitting & Crochet Guild:
Vintage knitting publications including *Woolcraft*. These are available free for members from the Knitting & Crochet Guild. Contact:
collections@kcguild.org.uk

Making Glove Blockers at Home:
https://www.asatricosa.com/glove-blockers/

How to Knit Gloves:
Complete tutorial about knitting gloves in the round and taking measurements for personal fit:
https://nimble-needles.com/patterns/how-to-knit-gloves/

Staci Perry, VeryPink Knits:
All knitting techniques needed for gloves, plus YouTube video for glove knitting:
https://verypink.com/2011/07/21/learn-to-knit-gloves/

Sue Carne:
Flickr sanQR.
https://www.flickr.com/photos/siouxian/albums/

ACKNOWLEDGEMENTS

Thanks are due to the many people who have contributed to this book: family, friends, and many museum and collection professionals and volunteers have been an integral part of the work. Illustrations and images have been a particularly collaborative effort, but especial thanks are due to the following:

My illustrators: Jenny Ackroyd for her hand-drawn diagrams and maps; Hilary Diaper for her glove and book cover drawings; Bronwen Thomas for all the chapter opener drawings; and Geof Cunningham for the use of the frontispiece image.

My readers: Gordon Wilson, Hilary Diaper, Lesley O'Connell Edwards and May MacCormick.

Thanks must also be given to museum curators Fiona Rosher of the Dales Countryside Museum, Hawes, and Joanne Turner of the Dumfries Museum for providing custom images; and to Kadri Vissel, of the Estonian National Museum, for the use of images of their collections.

Thanks are also due to my 'Holy Hands' colleagues, Lesley O'Connell Edwards and Dr Jane Malcolm-Davies – Jane for input and images of the 'Sture' glove, and to her and Ana Ehn Lundgren of the Cathedral Museum Uppsala for permission for their use.

Also to fellow volunteers at the Collection of the Knitting & Crochet Guild, Slaithwaite, West Yorkshire, for support and information; images of items from the Knitting and Crochet Guild's Collection are reproduced with permission of the Guild.

In particular I would like to thank the following for providing images, or allowing the use of images free of charge:
Freddie Robins, UK
Kathrin Zutturi, Hofburg Museum, Brixen/Bressanone
Marcel Baurier, Cathédral Sainte-Marie of St Bertrand de Comminges

Carol Christiansen, Shetland Museum and Archives
Ilse Stap, Fries Museum
Alan and Vanessa Hopkins, The Hopkins Collection
May MacCormick, Sanquhar
William Dalgleish, Sanquhar
Laura Jõe, Estonia
Külli Jacobson, Estonia
Kristi Jõeste, Estonia
Riina Tomberg, Estonia
Anu Pink and Siiri Reimann, Estonia
Michele Poulin-Alfeld, USA
Nancy Bush, USA
Sue Carne, UK
Brynmor Watson, UK
Rodney Jagelman, Chairman of the Glove Collection Trust.
All other photographs © Angharad Thomas

With thanks to my test knitters Carla Bainbridge, Jen Kaines, Lin Malcolm, Gill Omer, Eileen Pritchett and Colleen Whyatt, who test-knitted the patterns and gave useful feedback.

Huge thanks must be given to the following companies for yarn support: Blacker Yarns (www.blackeryarns.co.uk); Cygnet Yarns Ltd (www.cygnetyarns.com); Kate Davies Designs (www.shopkdd.com); Jamiesons of Shetland (www.jamiesonsofshetland.co.uk); Louisa Harding (www.yarntelier.com) for cashmere to sample and photograph; and Lovecrafts (www.lovecrafts.com). Also to Jane Hull, Knitting & Crochet Guild volunteer, for the supply of specialist and unusual yarns, and thiscraftyoctopus for the stitch markers.

And lastly to my civil partner, Gordon Wilson, for his unwavering support, advice and input.

Any errors or mistakes are, of course, my own.

INDEX

A

adapting   12, 84–5, 93–7, **96**, 127
Allen, Mary   45, 58–63, **60**, 73, 94, 126–7, 138, 140
    in Knitting & Crochet Guild collection   62
    keeping the Mary Allen knitting tradition alive   61
    knitting a replica   61–3
    Pattern 3, inspired by   65–9, **65–8**
    portrait   **59**
    see also Dales gloves *and* Dent
anatomy of a glove   12, **12**

B

bespoke gloves   100–2, **101**
blockers   24–5, **24**, 141
blocking   24–5, 64

C

casting off   96–7
casting on   21–6, **21**, **26–7**, 29, 65–6, 86, 102
    at the cuff   23, 62
    for finger and thumb constructions   24
    guidance on internet   25
    two-colour   25, 63–4, 110, **110**
    see also design
Centre de Documentació i Museu Tèxtil, Barcelona   40, 50, 120,
    122, 123, 139
chart, knitting from a   **51**, 61–2, **61**, 64
circular knitting   *see* techniques for glove knitting: knitting in the
    round
collections
    knitted gloves in   117–27
    on-line   36–7, 39–40, 42, 48, 123
    see also Glove Collection Trust, Knitting & Crochet Guild *and*
        museums
colour   15–16, **15–16**, 42, 49, 55–6, 63–4, 71, 102, 115
    and colourwork in Estonian gloves   81–7, **82–7**, 108–9, **108**
    and moodboards   103–6, **105**
    and sewing-up thread   22
    playing with colour   95, **95**
    see also chart, design *and* patterns in this book

cotton
    gloves   42, 119–20, **121**, 126–8, **126–7**
    liturgical gloves   35
    yarn 15, **15**, 75, 85, 106
cuff   12, 14–15, 21, **21**, 23, **26**, 29, 71
    and design   94–5, 99, 108–10, **109–10**
    chart   51, **51**
    Estonian   **19**, 48–9, **49**, 82–8, **82–7**, 110, **110**, 112
    fringed   43–4, **43**, 46, 48, 85, **87**
    fringed Estonian wedding cuff   87, **87**
    gauntlet   9, 11, 36–7, 40–2, 92, 120, **120**, 125–6, **125**
    magic loop method   20, **20**, 23, 25
    mystery cuff, Dutch gloves with   42–3, **42**
    Sanquhar   71, **72–3**
    sideways knitted   83, **83**
    with embroidery   36–7, **36–7**, 43, 82, 85, 120, **120–1**
    see also casting on, stages in knitting a glove *and* techniques for
        glove knitting
customizing   65, 71, 93–4, 98, **99**, 100, 112

D

Dales   7, 44–6, 56–63, 65
Dales Countryside Museum, Hawes   45–6, **59**, 59–61, 117, 142
Dales gloves   56, 58–63, **58**, **60**, **62–3**
    patterns   58, **61**
    rural knitting industry   44–5
    see also Allen, Dales Countryside Museum, Dent, museums, *Old
        Handknitters of the Dales and* Yorkshire
Dent   45, 58–61, **59**
Dent gloves   62–3, **62–3**
    story of the Dent gloves   62–3
    see also Allen
design
    design sheets   107, **107**
    for glove knitters   93–115
    inspiration   102
    process   102
    the design brief   106
    what is 'designing'?   94
    see also lookbooks, moodboards *and* templates

direction of knitting 14
    see also sideways knitted gloves
Dumfries Museum 47, **47**, 117, 123, 140, 142

E
Estonia 47–9, **48**, 81–7, **81**
    crafts and culture 81–2
Estonian gloves 81–7
    colours and colourwork 86
    entrelac cuff 82–3, **82–3**, 86–7
    features of a typical Estonian glove 85
    knitting in 24, 47–9, 55
    sideways knit cuffs 83, **83**
    techniques used in knitting 86–7, **86–7**
    what does an Estonian glove look like? 82–7, **82–7**
    see also cuff
Estonian National Museum 48–9, **49**, 81–2, **81**, 85, **85**, 123, 140, 142

F
finger gusset or fourchette 12, **12**, 44, 70–1, **72**
fingers **27–8**
    and stages in knitting a glove 112
    pleated **72**
    pointed 12, 50, **50**, 120, **120**
    see also anatomy of a glove, casting on *and* patterns in this book
fingertips, shaping and finishing 24, 64, **72**
finishing 24, **28–9**, 30–1, 53, 64–5, 69, 78, 80, 91, 114
    pressing, blocking and washing 24, **24**
    sewing in the ends and neatening the work 24, 114
Forsyth, Mary 73, **74**
Framework Knitters Guild 114
Fries Museum, Leeuwarden 42–3, 142

G
garter stitch 83–4, 87, 110, 124
Glove Collection Trust, the 9, 37, 39, 117–23, **118–22**, 123, 139, 142
    and liturgical gloves 37, **118–21**
    silk gloves – the same but different 39–40
gloves
    and artists 9–10, **10**, 56, 119
    anatomy of 12
    as form of clothing 33–4
    as gifts 7, 47
    as tokens of love 7, 9, 38–9
    beaded 120, **121**
    construction 112, **112**
    ecclesiastical 39–40, 118, **118**, 119, **120**
    expressing feelings – exploring relationships 9
    fingerless 11–12, **87**, 96, **96**
    for a musician 100–2, **101**
    knitted flat with a gauntlet 125, **125**
    language of 7, 9–11
    purposes of 7
    sideways knitted *see* sideways knitted gloves
    silk 35–40, **35–7**, **39–40**, 50, **50**, 60, **60**, 118–20, **118**, **120**, 122, **122**
    types of handcovering 11, **11**
    using lace 9, 36, 40, 48, 87, 87, 119–20, **119–20**
    white 7, 87
    words and phrases for 7
    see also liturgical gloves, Sanquhar gloves *and* types of glove

guilds and glove making 38
    see also Knitting & Crochet Guild *and* Worshipful Company of Glovers of London
'Gunnister Man' gloves 40–2, **41**
    from Gunnister burial **41**
    reconstruction **41**

H
Hartley, Marie 46, 56, 58–9, **58**, 137
    see also Ingilby *and* Old Hand-Knitters of the Dales
Hawksley, Rozanne 9, 137, 139
hints, before you start 29
historical and notable gloves
    Brixen/Bressanone 35–6, **36**, 142
    de Courpalay, Pierre **34**, 35
    de Foix, Pierre 36, **37**
    Dutch gloves from 1783 42, **42**
    Fray Agustin Lopez 40, **40**
    'Gunnister Man' gloves (original and reconstruction) 40–2, **41**
    hiatus in the glove record 42
    Lord Howick's gloves 43–4, **43**
    M. Pearson's gloves **58**
    Marianne Clarke's gloves 43, **43**
    nineteenth-century 44–8, 56, 58, 73, 76, 81, 98
    of G. Walton 44, **44**, 46, 58
    S. Hunter 46, **46**, 62, 135
    'Saint Remi' gloves in Saint Sernin 35–6, **35**
    St Adalbert 14, 138
    story of the Dent gloves 62–3
    Sture glove, the 38–9, **39**
    see also gloves, ecclesiastical *and* liturgical gloves
history of knitting
    emergence of 'true' knitting through gloves 33
    gloves as a form of clothing 33
    introduction 34
    liturgical gloves 35
    see also The Old Hand-Knitters of the Dales 56–8
Holy Hands research project 38, 117, 123, 139, 142
Hopkins Collection 43, **43**, 142

I
Ingilby, Joan 46, 56, 58–9, **58**, 137
    see also Hartley *and* Old Hand-Knitters of the Dales
internet 17, 23
    resources for glove knitting 25

J
Jacobson, Külli **83–4**, 84, 142
Jõeste, Kristi **82**, 83, **83**, 85, **87**, 137

K
Kettle, Alice 9, 10, 141
knitting a glove
    process 28–9
    starting out 29–30
    techniques for knitting in two colours 63–4
    see also needles and techniques for glove knitting
Knitting & Crochet Guild (KCG) 62, 65, 77, 97, 104, 140, 141, 142
    and Dent gloves 62–3, **62–3**
    database 123–4

glove blockers **24**
items in KCG Collection **19, 24, 55, 62, 70–1**, 104
the KCG Collection 123–7, **123–7**
knitting in the round *see* techniques for glove knitting
knitting sheaths or sticks **45**
knitting software 102, 107, 114

L

liturgical gloves **32**, 35–7, **35–7**, 39–41, **39–41**, 71
characteristics of 36
Holy Hands research project 38, 117, 123, 139, 142
their survival 35
see also gloves, ecclesiastical *and* Glove Collection Trust
lookbooks 106, **106**, 141
looping 34–6, **34–5**
Lord Howick's gloves 43–4, **43**

M

MacCormick, May, Sanquhar glove expert **71**, 73, 75, **75**, 77, 142
machine knitting 14, 38, 62, 75–6, 96, 118
and sideways knit gloves 14
moodboards 103–5, **103–5**
digital 105
tools and materials for 103–5
mittens 11–12, **42**, 48–9, 75, 81–2, 96–7, **96**
museums
Centre de Documentació i Museu Tèxtil, Barcelona 40, 50, 120, 122, 123, 139
Dales Countryside Museum, Hawes 45–6, **59**, 59–61, 117, 142
Dumfries Museum 47, **47**, 117, 123, 140, 142
Estonian National Museum 48–9, **49**, 81–2, **81**, 85, **85**, 123, 140, 142
Fries Museum, Leeuwarden 42–3, 142
Imperial War Museum, London 10
Leicester Museums and Galleries 43, **43**
National Museum of Scotland 41, **41**
Tolbooth Museum, Sanquhar 76, **76**, 123, 139
Wordsworth Trust, Grasmere 44, **44**, 58, 61–2, 126
see also collections

N

nalbinding 34–5, *see also* looping
needle gauge 21–2, 22
needles for knitting gloves 14, 17–21
circular 19–21, **19–20**, 23, 25–6, **26**, 29, 64, **64**, 112
double-pointed 18–19, **18–19**, 22–3, 25, 45, 83, 86, 127
flexible double-pointed 21, **21**
interchangeable 19
needles for sewing up 22, 24
North of England and Yorkshire 44

O

Old Hand-Knitters of the Dales 56–8
illustrated covers of editions **57**

P

patterned gloves 55–91
in Estonia 81–91, **82–7**
in Scotland 70–80, **70–6**
in Yorkshire 56–69, **55, 58, 60, 62–4**

patterns
colour patterns, working out 23, 102
for knitting Dales gloves 61–2
for knitting Sanquhar gloves 74–7
for sideways knitting 14
free on the internet 25, 97, 140
sampler-type 43–4, **43**
why knit a replica? 61
see also adapting, customizing *and* patterns in this book
patterns in this book
Pattern 1: Plain Inspired 30–1, **30**
Pattern 2: Inspired by History 50–3, **50**
Pattern 3: Inspired by Mary Allen 65–9, **65**
Pattern 4: Inspired by Alba 77–80, **77**
Pattern 5: Boreal Inspiration 88–91, **88**
Pattern 6: Vintage Inspiration 128–32, **128**
Platt Hall 10, *see also* Kettle
Prince of Wales *see* Sanquhar patterns
process of knitting a glove 26–9

R

Ringwood gloves 126–8, **126–7**
Robins, Freddie 10, **10**, 141–2

S

Saint Bertrand de Comminges, Cathédral Sainte-Marie 36–7, **36–7**, 142
samples 108, **108**
Sanquhar gloves 46–7, **47**, 70–7, **70–6**
patterns for 74–7, **74–6**
Tolbooth Museum, Sanquhar 76, **76**, 123, 139
tools and materials for 76
what is a Sanquhar glove? 70–4
Sanquhar patterns 70–3, **70–3**, 75, 104
Cornet 73, **73**
customized 71, **71**, 98–102, **98–101**
Duke 47, **47**, 70–1, **71**, 73, 75, 99, 140
Midge and Flea or Fly 62, **62**, 71, 75, 140
modern logic symbols 99, **99**
Prince of Wales 71, 75, 140
QR code 100, **100**
Shepherd's Plaid 71, 75, 140
see also MacCormick, May *and* Sanquhar gloves
Scotland 44, 46–7
National Museum of Scotland 41, **41**
textile production in southern Scotland 46
see also Dumfries Museum, Sanquhar gloves *and* Sanquhar patterns
second-glove syndrome 21, **21**
self-care 23, 29
sewing up 22, 24
see also finishing *and* needles for sewing up
Shakespeare 7
Shetland 18, 40, **40**
Shetland Museum 41–2, **41**
see also 'Gunnister Man' gloves
sideways knitted gloves 14, 124, **124**, 126
cuffs 83
in garter stitch 14, 83
significance of gloves 9
silk *see* gloves, silk *and* yarn

size   24–5, 63, 96–7
    considering the finished size   25
    discussion of   97
    does size matter?   25
    working out size and construction 111–14
Skelton, John Alexander   96
speckle pattern and stitch 42, 64, 66, 77–8, **77–8**, 88, **88**, 90, **90**
stages in knitting a glove   112–4
starting out knitting gloves   14–29, 102
    handy hints   29
stash   *see* yarn
Stratford, Audrie   124
Sture glove, the   38–9, **39**, 142
swatches   104, 108–12, **108–9**, **111**, 114–15

T
techniques for glove knitting   23
    casting on at the cuff   23
    casting on for finger and thumb constructions   24
    illustrated sequence   26–9
    increasing in the round   23
    joining into the round at the cuff   23
    knitting in the round   23
    knitting in two colours   63–4
    magic loop method for cuff   20
    making notes   22
    pick up and knit (joining)   24
    plain gloves   23
    shaping fingertips and finishing   24
    taking stitches off needles and onto threads   23
    see also chart, knitting from a
template, hand   107, **108**
templates   23, 107–8, **108**, 111
tension or gauge   25, 76–7, 97, 102, 109–11, **111**
texture   12, 95–6, **95**, 102, 126–8
thumb
    asymmetrical   **13**, 14, 113
    choice of   113
    construction of   12–14, **13**, 112–14
    gusset   12, **12**, 14, **26**, 29, 42–3, 62, **62**, 70, **72**, 85, 102, 112–13, 126
    peasant   **13**, 14, 39, **39**, 44, 83, **83**, 85, 113, 126, **126**
    position of the thumb   12–14, **13**
    symmetrical   **13**, 14
Tomberg, Riina   **84–5**, 84, 142
tools and materials for moodboards   103, **103**
tools for glove knitting   **22**
    knitting bags   22, **23**
    needle gauge   21
    Sanquhar gloves   76
    stitch markers   22
    see also templates
Turnau, Irene, knitting before mass production   42, 137

types of glove
    hand covering types   11
    hand warmers   11, 96, **96**
    looking like samplers   43–4, **43**
    mittens   11–12, 38, **42**, 48–9, 55, 75, 81–5, 96, **96**, 97, 122
    wrist warmers   11–12, 87
    see also adapting patterns *and* Sture

U
Uppsala Cathedral   38–9, **39**, 142

V
Victoria & Albert Museum   **10**, 15, 36, 139
vintage
    Sanquhar glove   71–3, **72**
    yarns   17, **17**, 77, 97

W
Wales   7, 44, 81, 103
white gloves   7
wool
    and its relations   15, **15**
    blends and mixtures   16
    hand-spun yarn   16
    sheep breeds   16, **16**
    see also yarns
Wordsworth Trust, Grasmere   44, **44**, 58, 61–2, 126
Worshipful Company of Glovers of London, the   9, 37–8, 117–23
    see also Glove Collection Trust

Y
yarn
    artisan   **16**
    blends and mixtures   16, **16**
    cotton   15, **15**, 35, 42, 75, 85, 106, 119, **119**, 120, **121**, 126–7
    for glove knitting   15, **15**
    information sources on yarn production   17
    silk   15, **15**, 20, **20**, 25, 55, 60–1, 95, 106, 110
    stash   95, 98, 105
    substituting   97
    type of yarn and how it is spun   17
    vintage   17
    woollen and worsted yarns   17, **17**
    see also wool
Yorkshire   44–6
    knitting methods in rural areas   45
    nineteenth-century gloves in   46
Yorkshire Dales   *see* Dales

Z
Zimmerman, Elizabeth   14, 124, 137